OTHER BOOKS BY STACEY MAY FOWLES

Infidelity (novel, 2013)

Fear of Fighting
(novel with illustrations by Marlena Zuber, 2008)

Be Good (novel, 2007)

STACEY MAY FOWLES

Baseball Life Advice

Loving the Game That Saved Me

McClelland & Stewart

Library and Archives Canada Cataloguing in Publication is available upon request

Published simultaneously in the United States of America
by McClelland & Stewart, a Penguin Random House Company

Library of Congress Control Number is available upon request

ISBN: 978-0-7710-3871-6
ebook ISBN: 978-0-7710-3872-3

Book designed by CS Richardson
Jacket images: diamond © enterlivedesign/Shutterstock.com;
grass © Hudiemm/Getty Images

Typeset in Adobe Caslon by M&S, Toronto
Printed and bound in the USA

McClelland & Stewart,
a division of Penguin Random House Canada Limited,
a Penguin Random House Company
www.penguinrandomhouse.ca

1 2 3 4 5 21 20 19 18 17

Penguin Random House

For my dad

"The game proceeds at just the right pace: the one detractors call boring. It is gentle and relaxed, full of spaces for reflection or conversation, quiet moments in which to relish a play just made or a confrontation about to occur. What's the rush? The longer the game, the more there is to enjoy.

It's hard to understand people who hate baseball, but easy to pity them."

ALISON GORDON

Foul Balls: Five Years in the American League

CONTENTS

FOREWORD

I'll forever remember growing up an Atlanta Braves fan in Nashville, Tennessee, listening to the broadcasts with my dad in the front bench seat of his old blue Chevy Nova. The A/C didn't work and the sweltering summer heat would make even the steering wheel sweat, but I didn't care. The only thing I cared about was getting to listen to the games with my dad's arm around me, dreaming of being the next Dale Murphy or Steve Bedrosian. It was a safe place to dream and talk and hope. As time passed and my relationship with my dad became strained, I would often return to that place, where time seemed to stop except for the sweet noise of the crackling radio, my favourite Brave circling the bases after a home run, and the feel of my dad's strong arm holding me close. It brought me such peace.

I am forty-two years old now, in the twilight of my career, and frequently find myself reflecting on why baseball has meant so much to me. It is not the competition that holds the weight for me. It is not the game itself. It is not a strikeout, a win, or any statistical accomplishment, although I do find joy in those. It is the template of baseball that I am in love with. It is the pace of the game that allows for a deep relationship between people in the stands. It is the length of the season that demands a real investment in getting to know the players who play it. It is the opportunity it offers for redemption and hope, as the guy who struck out in the first inning gets the game-winning hit in the ninth, or the team that finished last the year before can win their division the next. It is the game of perpetual second chances as spring training rolls around every February. Baseball is a game that forces you to find your way through adversity at every turn. In what other profession can you fail seven out of ten times and be a Hall of Famer! You have to learn to deal with small failures in order to realize your full potential.

I believe that baseball is the most intimate of all sports. As a player, I spend 220 days a year with twenty-four other men. My teammates become my family. When my dad passed away during the season in 2015, my teammates huddled around me at my locker, toasted my dad, and I hugged every one of them to a man, with tears pouring down my face; no shame, no judgment. They were simply my twenty-four brothers who cared about the one that was hurting. And there are countless stories that mirror that one throughout baseball. That's not to say that these types of stories don't occur in other sports. It is simply that baseball offers a consistent opportunity to enter into a relationship with others, and that has been one of the great gifts the game has given me.

I first talked to Stacey May Fowles in March of 2013. She was interviewing me for a publication she was working for, about a children's book I had written. I've given literally thousands of interviews, but I could sense that this one was very different. What started out as a simple interview turned quickly into an intimate conversation about the parallels in our lives and the similar traumas we had endured. We must have talked for over an hour about what was both hard about our stories and wonderful about them as well. I was captivated by her humanity and sincerity. She talked about what the game of baseball and being a Blue Jays fan have meant to her, but she did it in a way that left me spellbound.

These essays take the reader on a rich journey. Stacey May Fowles writes with such passion, and challenges us to look beyond the stat sheet in order to drink deeply from a game that is so much more than the players who play it. She writes that baseball is "the one place I had always gone to for solace in the face of painful circumstances." It is this exact sentiment that I can connect with the most—that baseball is a sanctuary where one can find a temporary peace. Fowles's personal anecdotes about her relationship with the game make me thankful that in some small way I have been a part of the landscape of her life.

R.A. Dickey

AUTHOR'S NOTE

Early in the 2015 baseball season, I noticed that the responses players were giving in postgame scrums occasionally provided unexpected insight into how we could all better live our lives. Like most fans, I had long believed that the game provides a template for how to live a happier, more fulfilling existence, but this acute realization inspired a personal project—compiling these sometimes-thoughtful quotes and distributing them to the masses.

Thus, *Baseball Life Advice* was born, a humble weekly newsletter that offered, among other things, an inspiring quote from a player, manager, or sportswriter that could be applied to our experiences off the field. On May 1, 2015, I sent out the very first edition to 111 subscribers, featuring a piece of silver-lining optimism care of Toronto Blue Jays manager John Gibbons: "We didn't get a lot of hits, but it sure felt like we hit some balls hard." (The Jays lost that game, 4–1, to the Red Sox, and the team was, at the time, last in the division.)

Over the months and years that followed, the newsletter has evolved and its followers have grown into the thousands. It has become a place where I share my work and my thoughts on the game, and where I connect with a variety of fans from across the league, but my initial mission to bring a tiny nugget of baseball life advice to readers remains the same. Some of these collected quotations appear throughout this book, and I hope they bring a little joy and insight into your life—just like they did for me.

BASEBALL LIFE ADVICE

IT'S ENOUGH THAT WE'RE HERE: THOUGHTS ON BASEBALL AND RECOVERY

The month I started writing this piece, I got into my first bike accident. The only really notable thing about my tumble was that it was long overdue, a collision with concrete being a rite of passage for any long-time city cyclist. All told it was a standard spill, the kind bike commuters endure and then speak of like a war story over beers with the uninitiated. Turning left into an intersection, my front tire caught in the streetcar tracks and I was thrown forward, landing on my palms and knuckles, then on my (thankfully helmeted) head, and then on my knees. Aside from some colourful bruises, a ruined pair of jeans, and worry from an overly concerned mother, I came out pretty much unscathed.

Kindly strangers who saw me fall pulled me to my feet and helped collect my belongings, wheeling my bent bike to the safety of the sidewalk. A University of Toronto student scrambled into traffic for my phone, wallet, and earbuds, and placed them all in my scraped hands, repeatedly asking if he should call an ambulance. A hot-dog vendor kindly offered me a free bottle of water. A woman joked that my just-purchased bottle of Prosecco made it out alive. I popped it later to celebrate how lucky I was that I did, too.

In the thick adrenalin of the moment, my hands streaked with black road-filth and blood, I remember having an entirely misplaced, hilarious thought after I collected my shaky self off the asphalt.

What if it had been worse? What if I couldn't go to baseball games anymore?

I've been going to see the Toronto Blue Jays since the early 1980s, when they were still playing at Exhibition Stadium and I was in diapers (which is more fact than brag). But it wasn't until the end of 2011, during a period of particular hardship, that I developed this inexplicable, full-gut longing and heartsickness for it all, the kind of love that means baseball is the first thing I think of in the morning, or even when splattered on the pavement. The emotion the game stirs in me is like an itch I can't scratch, a feeling I'll never really understand. The closest I've gotten is likening it to a brand-new crush that doesn't fade as the years pass—a forever-unrequited, deep-bone affection that spurs me onward instead of demoralizing me. Most of the time, I'm simply happy that I care about something that much.

Since 2011, the boys of summer have come to dictate

how I navigate most of my days, even the ones during the long, dark offseason when diamonds across North America are piled with snow. I scour the news for their stories daily, these strangers who've devoted their lives to a child's game. I've learned how former Toronto Blue Jay Mark Buehrle loves his pit bulls, how Texas Ranger Josh Hamilton bounced back from drug and alcohol addictions, how Seattle Mariner Adam Lind's wife is from Scarborough, Ontario. I check up on the stats of my favourite hitters and pitchers, sneak game updates on my phone at social events, and cultivate a small community of similar devotees to share stories with.

I'm not in any way resentful of baseball's strange grip on me, but rather am grateful, and would even go as far as to say that my need for it saved my life.

In 2011, at the age of thirty-two, I suffered my first full-blown depression, the kind that made the contents of my fridge confusing and made it impossible for me to want to do anything other than stay in bed. I'd experienced mental illness before, having been diagnosed with generalized anxiety disorder in my mid-twenties, but the irrational fear of dying that was always present in my buzzing, twitchy brain suddenly gave way to a terrible, terrifying desire for it. I recall quite vividly a moment, while sitting in the shower, that I craved death's release, and the stray thought scared me so completely that I got myself into crisis counselling immediately.

Thankfully, I had long been adept at projecting the illusion of togetherness. My lack of wellness often feels abstract, even separate from me, like I've been watching someone else suffer through the thick fog of sadness that first overtook me during the 107th World Series. (In case you were wondering, the Cardinals beat the Rangers in seven.) But during that year's offseason I faced a long-overdue diagnosis of post-traumatic stress disorder—the culmination of life events that started with a sexual assault I endured as a teen. I've since been in and out of rape-counselling sessions, intensely questioned by a psychiatrist, prescribed various drugs by doctors, and attempted mindfulness, meditation, acupuncture, deep breathing, and even boxing. I've been claustrophobic, agoraphobic, anxious, depressed, and viciously afraid of a long list of mundane things and activities that many would find laughable. Crowds scare me. Subways scare me. Elevators scare me. Sitting too far from an exit scares me. Walking down the street, day or night, scares me. Yet through all of it, the one thing that has buoyed me is baseball: its tiny dramas, its compelling backstories, its Powerade-drenched victories, its hot, sweaty midsummer slumps.

Crowd-pleasing Munenori Kawasaki's first home run as a Toronto Blue Jay. Storied Derek Jeter's last at-bat with the New York Yankees. Washington Nationals pitcher Max Scherzer dedicating every start to a brother lost to suicide. Steer-roping Madison Bumgarner leading the San Francisco Giants to a World Series championship. A rookie's first major-league hit with his whole family cheering from the stands. A warm hug shared between a pitcher and catcher after a game-winning strikeout. The dugout-clearing joy of a walk-off home run. A bat flip that became legendary.

Baseball became "my thing," and its stadiums my church, a place to pray in times of hopelessness, the source of a solace I couldn't find elsewhere. I never feel more human, or more sane, than I do inside a ballpark.

Admittedly, it's hard for me to write about baseball and the feelings it conjures. I've written about countless difficult topics—my experience with sexual assault and subsequent mental health issues included—but when I sit down to explain this rather mundane thing I adore, how it cured what was ailing me, I always struggle. Not only is it generally considered gauche in literary circles to write about what you deeply love, it's also incredibly difficult to do it well. Culturally, we seem to have confused cynicism for intelligence, meaning it's so much easier to dash off a disgruntled diatribe than it is to explain, in a compelling way, feelings of intense admiration. And how exactly do you explain how baseball cures a panic attack?

Beyond that, when I started writing about the game, I was unsure my voice would be welcomed—because my perspective comes from a place in the stands, and because I am a woman. I was uncertain whether there would even be a spot for me in this world where men and their "insider" observations and opinions make up the status quo.

I knew that my affection for the summer game could easily be dismissed as obsession, addiction, or even fetish, but for whatever reason, baseball has come to rule me: over the past five years it has become my everything; my hunger for it actually alters how I live my life. During a Toronto Blue Jays homestand, I feel this rising worry that I won't be able to attend every game in person, that I'll miss some vital moment at the stadium because I have to work or go to an obligatory event, or because I'll suddenly come down with a case of the flu. I'll decline invites, rearrange my schedule, and fail to eat properly because hot dogs and cans of Bud will be on offer at the Rogers Centre. I'll sleepily slump through work because last night's game went into extra innings, and I'll sneak glances at video of a day game at my desk because god forbid I miss an incredible play. Once I even walked out of my downtown office to slip into the stadium because it looked like maybe, just *maybe*, a pitcher was going to throw a no-hitter (which was of course broken up minutes after I arrived and bought a tall can).

Baseball is one of those things I was never told I should love. It wasn't passed down to me like some sacred family heirloom, and I didn't take it up because of a desperate need to fit in. In many ways, I chose it for myself. Throughout my life I've been told I should love certain books and films, certain bands and fashions. I've struggled to love jobs I've done, men I've dated, family members who were less than lovable. But unlike most people and things, baseball never asked anything of me, and no one ever demanded I be loyal to it. I never played it, my parents didn't strong-arm me into attending games, and I didn't have a social group that insisted it become an integral part of my life. In fact, I would say that I was largely discouraged from loving this pastime and culture—built for men and boys, fathers and sons—that's not always welcoming of my gender. There is no real template for loving baseball when you're a girl or a woman, so you have to fumble around a bit to make it your own. I like to think I truly love the game because it made itself hard to love and I embraced it anyway. Because of that, it belongs to me in a way nothing else does.

Now every March finds me, an unlikely pilgrim, making the sacred trip to Florida for spring training. I get in a tiny airport rental car to tour the ballparks of Lakeland, Clearwater, and Dunedin, to chat with aging snowbirds who call the state their part-time home. The list of major-league ballparks I've seen across the U.S. is growing—in the past five years I've crossed Yankee Stadium, Dodger Stadium, Angel Stadium, Fenway Park, Nationals Park, AT&T Park, Wrigley Field, U.S. Cellular Field, and the Oakland-Alameda County Coliseum off my list. I've bought programs, sipped summer shandy, and drunkenly waited out rain delays with welcoming fans from other towns. I've compared the quality of each park's hot dogs, and made it a tradition to buy the ball cap of each team I've visited. I've become a person I didn't know I had it in me to be—someone who's enthusiastic and takes pleasure in something simply for the sake of it.

And for someone who once found herself in depression's deep well, that's a glorious thing.

In recovering from mental illness, I've learned that structure is the key to any therapeutic process. When I was finally diagnosed with PTSD, baseball generously provided its nine-inning, 162-game scaffolding when I needed it the most. I revelled in the fact that its men play by a set of agreed-upon rules, that you can know what to expect, and that even the unexpected falls into a set framework—white lines drawn cleanly in Kentucky bluegrass.

Filling out a box score is like completing a cognitive behavioural therapy workbook: methodical and precise, soothing in its documentation of progress. Each inning is a unique chapter, and whatever happened in the second does not necessarily dictate what will happen by the seventh. Beyond that, the game's leisurely pace and lack of a running clock mirrors the lack of pressure necessary to progress through recovery. It only makes sense that, sprawled out on the pavement with a bent-up bike, I would be terrified to lose the one thing that always made me feel like I could get better.

For me—and I imagine for many others—baseball provides a soothing constancy. I suspect it's a similar relationship people have with religion, this idea that there is always something predictable, a doctrine to turn to, when it feels like there is nothing left. Baseball is hope. Baseball is narrative. Baseball is a thing to do when there's nothing to be done. And at the risk of hyperbole, the possibilities inherent in tomorrow's matchup give you a reason to go on. When you love the game this much, you inevitably come to measure your life in its ebbs and flows, in its fresh starts and postseasons, and in its thankfully reliable annual return. Each spring, without fail, it offers renewal: as everyone's stats roll back to zero, we're all given the opportunity to begin again. There's no guarantee that last year's champion will be triumphant; every hero will make room for another, and every underdog will be rife with potential.

There's something about the pace of play in baseball that suggests you have all the time you need, and something about the feeling it conjures that says, win or lose, it's enough that we're here. It's a long game and a long season, and it's always possible to heal what has been broken.

"This was a new recognition that perfection is admirable but a trifle inhuman, and that a stumbling kind of semi-success can be much more warming. Most of all, perhaps, these exultant yells for the Mets were also yells for ourselves, and came from a wry, half-understood recognition that there is more Met than Yankee in every one of us."

ROGER ANGELL

The Summer Game

"You don't have to look like an Under Armour mannequin to be an athlete. A lot of people probably think I'm not athletic or don't even try to work out or whatever, but I do. Just because you're big doesn't mean you can't be an athlete. And just because you work out doesn't mean you're going to have a twelve-pack."

PRINCE FIELDER

on posing nude for ESPN*'s 2014 Body Issue*

"I'm a team player, I'm a clubhouse guy. I try to keep everyone loose and I've been doing this since day one when I got to the big leagues, and I'm going to continue to do it, man. Life is too short."

DIONER NAVARRO

DIONER NAVARRO MADE THE ONE I LOVE LOVE BASEBALL

Just over ten years ago, I fell in love with a person who didn't like baseball.

Of all the possible problematic relationship dynamics, I know that this one doesn't even crack the top one hundred. In terms of spousal compatibility, I'm certainly one of the lucky ones. Having said that, this specific imbalance of personal interests has been a source of conflict in our day-to-day lives. In the marriage of two workaholics, downtime is precious, and because I want baseball to monopolize pretty much all of it—whether from the couch or at the stadium—we've often had to negotiate just how we're going to unwind.

Over the course of my marriage, I've been (rightfully) chided for checking the score during dinner with the in-laws, and for staring vacantly at my MLB.tv-equipped phone during what should be date night. Summer Saturday eating-locales usually have to come equipped with a television turned to a sports channel. Want Thai food for lunch? Too bad. The BBQ joint next door is showing the Jays vs. the Red Sox game and I hope you like ribs. You may want to go to the movies this Friday night, but sneaking a peek at my phone during an explosive CGI action sequence would simply be rude. Better to wait until we can rent it and watch at home so I can see how the Jays are faring against the Rays in the upper-right corner of the screen.

I'm also guilty of trying to cram a ballpark visit or two into almost all of our much-needed vacations. That glorious two-week road trip through California? It had a lot more to do with the Dodgers and the Giants than the Pacific Coast Highway and a tour through wine country. That weekend visit to D.C.? Sure the National Archives and the National Gallery of Art were lovely, but if I'm completely honest, Max Scherzer and Bryce Harper were the real draw. I've tried to covertly hunt down a baseball game to attend in Cuba during a short resort stay in the dead of a Canadian winter, and even attempted to seek out some university ball when we were in Las Vegas to get married. (I finally conceded to the sheer ridiculousness of that last one. I'm not a monster.)

It has taken a lot of hard work to get to the point where my husband is willing to give up some of his off-hours to go to a game. When we first started dating in the mid-2000s, he made it quite clear that he hated sports, and thought that they were an example of the worst kind of capitalism and hyper-masculinity that North America has to offer. He loathed the unthinking consumerism of fans mauling each other for the spoils of the T-shirt cannon, and was disgusted at the blind, shoving hero-worship of aggressive autograph-seekers. I'm actually kind of surprised I persisted in trying to get him to just relax and have some fun, given how firmly he resisted.

When we were in the very early stages of coupledom, I invited him along to a weekend afternoon game with my mom and dad. I assumed it would be a furtive bonding exercise, a way to get my family to connect with the person who I felt I had a future with, in a locale that always made me feel comfortable. As the four of us sat side by side in the 500 section of the Rogers Centre, my dad and I celebrated great moments from our favourite players, while my mom and my now-husband lamented that baseball was all just a boring slog. To be fair, I do actually think the two of them bonded over their amused disdain—they clinked their tall cans, lightly mocked our fandom, and by all accounts it was a successful afternoon with the future in-laws. But when I got a moment alone with him, I couldn't help but criticize: "Couldn't you have at least tried to pretend you enjoyed it?" While we're not really a couple who argues, I definitely delivered the silent treatment following that day's game.

I am convinced that, as the years went by, my husband did do his best to pretend to enjoy the game, and eventually that effort slowly evolved into admiration by proxy. There is something beautiful about watching someone you care about attempt to take on an interest of yours because he knows just how happy it makes you. After that initial false start, my husband came to understand deeply that the ballpark was a place where I felt safe and whole, and he took me there over and over again through the years to witness the happiness it brought me. If you "hate sports," it's a sacrifice to give up most of your free time to the tiny stadiums of Florida, or an Opening Day in New York, or a ballpark road trip in California, but he consistently obliged. I am so glad he finally came around, because there is no other person in the world I want to share a few beers at the game with more, even if the whole experience isn't as life-changingly blissful for him as it is for me.

That's why, during spring training 2015, when my husband told me that he thought he'd discovered his favourite player, I was elated. Anyone who has fallen head over heels in love with this game knows that the favourite player is a gateway drug. He's the first step in developing an all-encompassing obsession—a personality or a performance that suddenly makes you take note and find the will to care about the game, unaided by your wife's insistence that it's important. I can still remember the burgeoning baseball feelings that Devon White and Kelly Gruber gave me when I was in my early teens. Hell, 2015

American League MVP Josh Donaldson is probably solely responsible for a notable percentage of the current Toronto fanbase. For whatever inexplicable reason, you fall in baseball-love with one man in cleats, and through him the whole game opens up for you. You buy his jersey. You manically check his stats and defend him at every turn. Like Pavlov's dogs, you feel a thrill every time his walk-up music plays at the ballpark.

He's all yours—the living, breathing, human key to unlocking the game.

But my husband didn't go with an expected Blue Jays pick. He wasn't into Edwin Encarnación, or José Bautista, or that easy-to-love, sweet-faced Canuck Russell Martin. He didn't prioritize the fun, youthful energy of Marcus Stroman, or the intellectual, benevolent dad vibe of R.A. Dickey. No, he wanted to cheer the loudest for the lesser-celebrated Dioner "Little Pudge" Navarro. (As a diehard devotee of the not-so-popular Adam Lind, I was really in no position to judge.) In fact, he was quick to point out that Navarro fascinated him precisely because the backup catcher *wasn't* a star, because he seemed like a really nice guy, and because the steadfast, cerebral allure of the catcher appealed to my husband's personality. In short, Navarro seemed to defy everything about sports that my husband had professed to hate.

And thus, whenever Navarro came up to bat, my generally reserved partner-in-life would yell and cheer enthusiastically—the more comical chosen missives being "we should be friends!" and "we should hang out!" I watched as my husband exploded with unbridled joy during Navarro's base hits and home runs, and eventually I came to realize that maybe, thankfully, I wasn't the only baseball fan in our house anymore. He asked me more and more questions about the game, until soon he was providing me with details I didn't know. Navarro had brought my husband closer to baseball and, in turn, he had brought us closer together.

"I honestly can't explain why I liked him most, of all of the players, when I was first like 'that's my guy,'" my husband told me while washing dishes one night. "I guess he's like the anti-star. He's doesn't have the raw athleticism of Josh Donaldson. He doesn't belt out home runs like José Bautista or Edwin Encarnación. I like him because he's not the thing the game is known for. He's just this quiet dude. He's just a solid catcher who is actually shockingly good in a clutch."

My husband then questioned whether or not he was using the term *clutch* correctly.

It's true that in 2015, when my husband's love for him really flourished, Navarro wasn't exactly a stereotypical baseball hero. Backing up Russell Martin, he played in only fifty-four games, and had only 192 plate appearances. He hit five (very fun) home runs, twenty RBIs, and batted a pretty average .246. But he captured my husband's imagination regardless, just as his smiling face compelled the gleeful adoration of an entire playoff-intoxicated fanbase. I mean, how could you not be charmed by someone who had enough perspective to laugh and clap when position player Cliff Pennington threw a strike on his first pitch in the top of the ninth inning during a 14–2 ALCS loss to Kansas City?

It's actually not all that surprising that Navarro, although not a high-profile baseball celebrity, would sneak stealthily into my husband's otherwise sports-hating heart—this is a ballplayer who wears the number 30 because that was the day in September 2003 when his wife survived a cerebral aneurysm after being given a 5 per cent chance of survival. He's so grounded and down-to-earth that he loves to grab a pregame meal at the hot dog stands around the Rogers Centre: "Polish sausage," he told Kristina Rutherford of Sportsnet. "Then I put on onion, bacon, hot relish, ketchup, and mustard. I eat there maybe once a series." And I'm sure his status as an animal lover doesn't hurt either. (Over the years, Navarro has been reported to have two dogs, two birds, a chameleon named Jeffrey, a lizard named Tyke, and a pig named Sassy who he "treats like a princess.")

When Navarro signed a one-year deal with the White Sox in December 2015, I worried that my husband's love affair with the game would go with him. Would this be the end of his enthusiasm for baseball, an enthusiasm I had so desperately longed for all those years? Instead, he suggested we go ahead and visit the catcher in Chicago—a sweltering June game that featured both a miraculous in-the-park home run, care of former Blue Jay Brett Lawrie, and a 10–8 win for the Jays. My husband may have (shock! horror!) worn a White Sox cap for the duration of the game, but it was a genuine thrill to see him cheer for his personal fave all over again. Sure, we visited the Art Institute of Chicago on that trip as part of our usual tit-for-tat vacation exchange, but on this particular excursion it felt like he was really looking forward to going to the ballpark to see his hero.

I have Navarro to thank for the fact that my husband comes home with baseball stories and stats, trade news and game theories, and that we can finally, truly share this thing I love so much. He may not love it the same way I do, but he's found his own way to engage with it after years of thinking sports, and the sometimes-toxic culture that surrounds them, just weren't for him. (No small feat, Mr. Navarro.)

When the news broke in August 2016 that Navarro was returning from the White Sox to the wide-open arms of the Toronto Blue Jays, baseball feelings abounded. On social media, fans posted and reposted that classic photo of the catcher sucking on a cigar in a borrowed cop hat, taken after the Blue Jays won the 2015 ALDS. Blue Jays players themselves greeted him with hugs and gleeful shouts of "Navvy!" In an often-critical fan climate, I actually didn't see one negative online reaction to the acquisition, the celebration less about stats and more about how good he makes us feel about the game.

The fanbase was definitely excited, but for me the acquisition was far more personal. When my husband sent me an "um, did we bring Navarro back?" text, I didn't think about what Navarro would contribute to the prospects of my October-bound team. Instead, all I could think about was how happy seeing him back on that lineup card would make the person I love.

ONLY JUST MEN

On May 7, 2013, I had some pretty memorable realizations about baseball. About its risk, its fallibility, and its humanity. About what matters, and what doesn't. Many Blue Jays fans will remember that as the day pitcher J.A. Happ, during his first run as a Toronto Blue Jay, took a line drive from Tampa Bay Ray Desmond Jennings to the head, and suffered a contusion and a laceration to his left ear as a result.

I'll admit that, while watching Happ's 2016 success, I've been thinking a great deal about that game from three years ago. That's not because I'm a sadist or a masochist, but because for whatever reason it speaks to me about the nature of pitching, and how our personal relationships with players and teams evolve over time. It was a highly emotional and communal moment in context, and now it exists as a meaningful past detail in the rise of a pitcher's career.

Pitchers are gifted with the rare ability to be present in the moment, to stand unflinching and focused, with their fear turned off while the world buzzes around them. For those of us who dread exposure, anticipate failure, worry about pain, or simply don't want to be looked at, a determined man alone on the mound is easy inspiration. The pitcher suffers heartache and humiliation, and knows self-satisfaction and victory, all the while being nakedly visible at the centre of the game. If you think about it too deeply, it makes you dizzy with metaphor.

I've always had a great affection for pitchers for this very reason—I've even read books on the mental art of pitching in the hope that they would quell my own irrational anxieties. Pitchers bring solace to so many of us because, regardless of the outcome, the man who throws the ball comes back to perform again. When he fails, it is a slow, painful, drawn-out affair, and he suffers the mortifying process in full view of millions, nodding politely when he's pulled from the game. My heart always aches when the pitching coach, catcher, and infielders converge on the mound, when they ask him what's wrong and why things aren't working. It seems impossible that anyone could steady himself so consistently and never visibly fall apart. He takes the shame gracefully, and he chooses to do so over and over again.

In 2013, Happ was certainly choosing to come back again after humiliation. For the Toronto Blue Jays, the season was characterized primarily by crushing disappointment, a run that began with blockbuster trade–induced great expectations and ended with the team at 74–88 (and last place in the division). By the time Happ suffered that injury at Tropicana Field, he was already regarded as untrustworthy on the mound—on May 2 he'd fallen apart against the Red Sox, walking seven before being pulled in the fourth. Oddly, I still remember what he looked like after he exited that game. I have a distinct memory of an extended shot of him soul-searching in the Rogers Centre dugout, ghost-faced and staring off into the distance as fan commentary on his myriad failings flooded every available outlet. Pieces subsequently appeared with headlines like "Happ's free passes, command issues sink Blue Jays," and "Blue Jays postseason hopes already fading."

"I made it tough on myself," he told the media, attempting to explain all those walks he surrendered in just a handful of innings.

But on May 7, Happ came back to the mound again, and in the moments before his now infamous injury, things at the Trop were tied 1–1 with one out in the bottom of the second. I still have a really hard time watching the video of the sudden ball-to-skull shot that followed, not only because of how visceral my immediate reaction to it is, but also because of how all the emotions around that game still resonate with me more than three years later; the image of that ball hitting him is stuck in my mind on a haunting loop. It's a kind of baseball hazard we don't think about all that often—the possibility of real damage remote in a game that prides itself on its lack of aggression and collision. Baseball is a slow, gentlemanly beast, or so says the mythology. We're foolishly lulled into thinking that it's just strains and sprains and tight shoulders, that all the potential concussions are left to those other, more brutish sports.

At the time, I could only watch the actual hit to Happ with the sound turned off, unable to stomach the sickening thud of the thing. But even on mute, the moment broke me. After impact, the ball was still bizarrely in play while Happ lay on the ground, with two runners scoring on Jennings's hit, and Happ's teammates struggling with a compulsion to run to his aid from the dugout before time-out was finally called. There was blood on his hand from touching the wound, blood on the mound where he rested. Jennings was visibly shaken, covering part of his face with his jersey (the pair later connected, with Happ conveying that he understood it wasn't his fault, and Jennings presumably feeling less guilty about the whole awful thing). R.A. Dickey later told reporters that he immediately started praying. Adam Lind said the energy was "very sad."

While we all watched in groping fear, I was struck most by the way the stadium of 10,000 was impossibly still, with fans on their feet, and players in the dugout with their faces in their hands. The whole scene was a stark reminder that this sport we love and share is a burden carried by those who play it, that ballplayers take punishment so that we can have those precious few hours of escape, so that we can take a break. Baseball is a way for us to look away from life, and players give up their bodies in service to that impulse. Yes, they are very well-paid, superhuman stars, but in the end our dreams balance on the shoulders of men who are really only just men.

As Happ was carefully placed on a stretcher and wheeled away, he gave us a simple and promising wave. Brad Lincoln came in to replace him. The Jays were losing, and Lincoln steeled himself for the two outs necessary to bring an end to the horrible inning.

What unfolded was the game that narrative fans had been longing for—in the top of the eighth the Jays came back to tie the Rays, and in the ninth they scored the go-ahead and an insurance run to spare. The pitcher is brutally injured, and the team rallies back to win it, of course, for him. *Win it for Happ.*

After that game, Happ ended up on the fifteen-day disabled list, and then went to the sixty-day as he recovered from a skull fracture, a sprained right knee, and hearing loss. The interviews he gave in recovery emphasized how lucky he was. "It looks like I moved just a little bit," he said of the split-second moment. "I don't remember doing that, but it looks like it was just enough to where [the ball] must have caught me in a better spot, because I think it could have got me head-on."

After being traded at the end of 2014 for Michael Saunders, and spending some time pitching with the Mariners and then the Pirates, Happ is all ours again, something that many of us are probably surprised we're proud to say. When he was acquired at the end of November 2015, he was admittedly a big question mark, with some uncertain of his viability, while others cited his 1.85 ERA in eleven starts with the Pirates as a very good sign. Yet no one really anticipated how stunning he could actually be, or that, for a time, he'd end up with the best ERA on our roster and invoke (very different) headlines, like "J.A. Happ dominant in Blue Jays' win over Giants," and "J.A. Happ pitching like an elite lefty in his return to Toronto."

"He's a different cat now," manager John Gibbons explained.

Of course, this improvement is not a fluke or accident. As John Lott reported in the *National Post* when Happ was re-acquired, we're benefitting from Pirates pitching coach Ray Searage's ability to spot a now-corrected delivery flaw. "Searage helped him curb wasted motion and keep his body on a direct line to the plate while maintaining a higher arm slot," Lott wrote. The lefty's now elite numbers are a very happy case of how unpredictable baseball can be, and how it's never a good idea to bring your preconceived notions to its outcome.

Because I openly admit to being a narrative baseball fan, I feel comfortable saying how pleased I am to see

Happ's ascent, especially after seeing him suffer so acutely. For many fans, that 2013 game was unforgettable for all the worst kind of reasons, and Happ now seems poised to pitch unforgettably for all the right ones. His incredible good fortune in coming back from such a terrifying injury, coupled with his evolution into a top-tier 2016 pitcher, is both inspiring and fascinating.

What happened to J.A. Happ that Tuesday night in May 2013 forced us to acknowledge the unspoken agreement we have with players like him: He goes out there to win. We watch him to find solace and to leave our heads for a short time. And that tenuous relationship was marred in the second inning. If anything is clear it's that while we fuss and boo, or profess our grievances and annoyances about a team that is not performing as we were promised, this frustration is a fallacy in the face of an injury like the one Happ suffered. Though we often throw around the idea, there really is no sacred Church of Baseball—there are only the people who built it and the people who fill it, together. There is no actual magic, only the shared feelings of a community who believes in that magic.

And maybe it's only in these communal moments of suffering that we realize that all we really have is each other.

BRACE YOURSELF FOR DAVID PRICE

November 27, 2015

I don't have any sort of specialized knowledge when it comes to baseball's behind-the-scenes dramas. I'm okay with admitting that my "insider information" primarily comes from inside my heart. (Yeah, I'm kind of ashamed I wrote that, but it's the truth.) Like most fans, when it comes to free agency I try to keep up with the latest gossip, but mostly I wish someone would just text me an update when all is said and done. It would certainly be better than being forced to ride this scary emotional roller coaster we call "the offseason."

The world of baseball is pretty good at fostering rumour and conjecture, with "mystery teams" vying for your favourite players, and reporters eager to be the first to share any crumbs of news they're thrown. *Where is this player going? Who wants him to wear their uniform? How much is that big deal really going to cost?* Even though there isn't an MLB game to be played during the cold winter months, the hot stove of the offseason is pretty exciting in its own media sound bite–saturated way.

On that note, there have been a lot of thoughts, feelings, and numbers tossed around about Toronto Blue Jays pitcher David Price. The latest conjecture is that he'll likely go to the evil empire that is the Boston Red Sox because they have a gazillion more dollars than everyone else. The Red Sox, of course, are easy league-wide villains (excluding all those videos of David Ortiz talking to children or holding an adorable baby), so there's an element of "well, of course he'll go there" among online cynics, and a note of sadness among those who believe that loyalty should come before profit.

For the Blue Jays, Price was what people in the baseball world like to call "a rental." Yes, it's a cold and callous descriptor, but it's not far off the mark. At the trade deadline the Jays had a flicker of postseason potential, were actively looking for some elite pitching to complete their team puzzle, and acquired the top starter from the Detroit Tigers on July 30 as a result. In exchange, they gave up three left-handed pitching prospects, indicating a willingness to go all in on a playoff push. Sacrificing the future for the present was the organizational strategy, and one that many Jays fans, in all our excitement, were more than happy to celebrate.

At the time of the acquisition, Price had a strong 2.53

ERA with 138 strikeouts and 29 walks, and the Blue Jays were 51–51 and just two games out of a wild card spot. When I learned of the deal via my smartphone, I was lying in a Los Angeles hotel room bed, more than halfway into a two-week-long Californian baseball road trip to visit the A's, Giants, Angels, and Dodgers. With the breaking news staring me right in the face, I let out a kind of elated gasp-scream that caused my husband to knee-jerk believe something awful had happened. "David Price is a Blue Jay," I managed to blurt out before his concern snowballed. With this lofty acquisition, the championship-minded 2015 Blue Jays front office had given fans the precious midseason gift of hope, and our long-floundering team suddenly became actual contenders.

David Price ended up bringing so much more to the Blue Jays than high-quality pitching and the team's first postseason run in two decades. He was indisputably affable, charming, and kind-hearted, with a winning smile and an adorable French bulldog named Astro. He had a famous love of Rogers Centre popcorn, and gifted his teammates customized blue bathrobes and a pack of team scooters. (Dioner Navarro rode his to get hot dogs outside the stadium. José Bautista rode his home after a victorious Game Five of the ALDS.) Rental or not, everything Price offered made us fast friends, and when the 2015 season ended, we were unfazed by his subpar postseason performances. In truth, the idea of losing him from our roster hit harder than we perhaps initially imagined.

Sports analysts smarter than me have written extensively about what the Toronto Blue Jays would need to do—and how much they would have to pay—to make Price stay put, but as always, my preferred baseball beat is the more emotional side of the game. The hopeful (or perhaps naive) among us would like to think that Price is driven less by money and more by heart, and that he clearly loves the city and its fans enough to make a high price tag moot. According to one source, David Price and his agent stated that Toronto is "far and away" his top choice, and surely that enthusiasm to return to his white and blue uniform means something?

Toronto and Canadian baseball fans in general certainly launched a heartfelt campaign to make the pitcher stay. Some valiantly created a crowdsourced website called "Any Price for David"—a comprehensive online listing of all the things fans would be willing to do if he does decide to re-sign with the Jays. *If David Price stays in Toronto, I, Brad, agree to buy David and Astro a steak dinner at The Keg . . . If David Price stays in Toronto, I, Aaron, agree to run around naked . . .* and so on. Even if, at its core, baseball is a business, it doesn't hurt to believe in the romance of it all, and that maybe some things are more valuable than the almighty dollar.

Here's the thing about David Price: he is the baseball version of your teenage summer-camp boyfriend. He's that good-looking, nice guy who knows how to sail and tie knots. He is the lifeguard valiantly watching you swim laps in the lake, or the muscular high school senior who taught you how to paddle a kayak for the first time. He just showed up out of the blue in your life one day with all his adorable charm and thoughtful gifts, and put his arm around your shoulder when the sun was shining and the grass was green. He swept you right off your feet and left you breathless, and as time passed you couldn't imagine what your life was like before him. You laughed at all his jokes, felt safe in his embrace in the moonlight, and snuggled with him during movie night. During all of those thrilling moments, you were more than happy to think your love could and would last forever.

But c'mon kids, we all know you can't stay at summer camp indefinitely. The fun eventually has to come to an end, and the buses will arrive to drive everybody back to their hometowns. Everyone hugs you goodbye and promises they'll write every day. But we all know, deep in our hearts, that never really happens. The love fostered there, although beautiful and very real in the moment, doesn't last when the autumn chill sets in. In David Price's case, the fling began with an electric August 3 start at the Rogers Centre, and ended in the postseason during an October 23 ALCS Game Six loss.

The thing is, even after you're pulled apart by distance and circumstance, you never regret that life-changing, summer-camp boyfriend. He existed in a wonderful coming-of-age narrative, an escapist fantasy where everything was perfect among the pine trees. Even when you hear rumours that he's shopping around for a new crush, you're strangely okay because the entire set-up felt fleeting from the start, and you look back on your time with him with googly-eyed fondness rather than gut-wrenching, yearning remorse. "It was nice while it lasted," you longingly think to yourself while watching the season's first snow from your window. (Maybe I dated a really enigmatic and handsome sailing instructor in 1995, okay?) Though you hold out hope that we'll all be back together again next year, the reality is that, in life and in baseball, people pack their bags and they move on. We have to find a way to be okay with that, no matter how difficult it can be. And if you run into that summer crush again, it's not going to be weird and awkward, but end with a nice genuine moment of wishing him well, right?

All of this is to say that, despite the emotional turmoil that's brewing among the fanbase, I think I may have made peace with the idea that David Price will probably be leaving us. That doesn't mean I don't want him to stay in our uniform, from the bottom of my baseball-loving heart, or that I'm not exhausted by all the daily talk of his potential departure. To be honest, I'd rather this all be over sooner rather than later. But I can sheepishly accept that it's very likely we'll go our separate ways and he'll be really good at his job somewhere else. As with all of the memorable summer loves of my youth, I've come to terms with the fact that maybe this one just wasn't meant to last forever.

We'll always have those good times we shared from July to October, when we donned matching bathrobes and shared a bag of popcorn or two. We've pasted all those delightful memories into our collective scrapbooks. But that man deserves to get paid what he's worth, and if we can't give him what he's looking for, then someone else definitely should. Sure, parting ways with a beloved player is always a painful baseball reality to deal with, but true love always wants the best for those who come into our lives—even if that ultimately means saying goodbye.

The Boston Red Sox signed David Price to a seven-year, $217-million contract on December 4, 2015.

COMMUNING WITH THE BASEBALL GODS

In the late spring of 2014, as part of an annual event for Blue Jays season ticket holders, I finally got to take my shoes off and stand barefoot on the centre-field AstroTurf at the SkyDome. (When one is being romantic about that ballpark, it's hard to call it by its present name, the Rogers Centre.)

It was a childish, romantic thing that I've wanted to do for as long as I can remember. Yet, standing by the warning track, I felt both reluctance and overwhelming curiosity when finally given the opportunity to do so. I sneakily looked around and then slowly slipped off my sandals, stepping onto the springy plastic greenery and the sprinkling of fake brown dirt that carpets the expanse just beyond the bases. Part of me felt like I was going to get in trouble, that maybe I was doing something crass, disrespectful, and against the rules. Other fans wandered around me, shoes on and oblivious, none of them apparently harbouring a secret desire to feel the turf between their toes. Despite my hesitance and fear, I may have instinctively closed my eyes the moment the soles of my feet sunk in, as though I were communing with the baseball gods, connecting with a direct line to legend. (Yes, I realize they switch the turf out periodically; no need to nitpick here.)

I started watching baseball the way most of us do—my dad took me to the stadium before I was old enough to decide I wanted to go myself. In the late 1970s, my father was a relative newcomer to Canada. A long-time soccer fan, he developed an interest in baseball when the Blue Jays were introduced to the city of Toronto in 1977. I was born two years less a day after the team played their very first game at Exhibition Stadium, beating the White Sox, 9–5, in the April snow. (In true Canadian fashion, the Jays had to borrow a Zamboni from the NHL's Maple Leafs to clear the field of powder before the first pitch.) As both my father's and the city's interest in the team developed, it seemed only natural for him to take me along to enjoy nine innings in the sun.

My personal devotion to the sport certainly ebbed and flowed over the years I was growing up, before finally reaching the near-absurd intensity it sits at today. As a child I was probably more interested in stadium ice cream and French fries than I was in Dave Stieb or Lloyd Moseby, but a day at the park was always something easily loved. Even when I grew into an angsty, indifferent teen, more compelled by boy bands and school dances than deciphering the infield fly rule, I implicitly understood there was something hallowed about the entire experience, even if it was just the sacred fixed time spent with my shift-working father.

The true religion that is baseball showed its face to me on October 20, 1992, when I was thirteen years old. That age is formative enough for any girl, but it also happened to coincide with the first flush of a team I cared about winning something big. I remember sitting with my dad at the SkyDome, just beyond the wall in centre field. Like every life-defining moment, I also remember exactly what I was wearing that day: a fall-appropriate red plaid button-down shirt, blue jeans, and a pair of yellow lace-up boots.

At the time, I probably didn't fully comprehend what a rarity it was not only to see your team go to the World Series but to physically be there and watch them win. (Thank you, Dad.) Two decades' worth of subsequent seasons spent sipping overpriced beers in a nearly empty ballpark, repeating the sad old mantra "maybe next year," have made clear just how spoiled I was in my youth by the success of my team.

But on that day in 1992 I got to witness, in person, what has come to be known in Blue Jays circles as "The Catch."

With all due respect to Kevin Pillar's recent heroics, the capital letters signify the most famous glovework in franchise history, and I wield my being there as an insufferable badge of honour when debating pivotal sports moments with my peers. It's a status symbol, a boast that inspires awe and envy, and prompts retellings of the now-mythic events that transpired that evening.

With two men on and nobody out in the fourth inning, storied slugger David Justice—incidentally, once voted one of *People Magazine*'s 50 Most Beautiful People—launched a Juan Guzmán fastball deep in our direction. Jays centre fielder Devon White was at medium depth at the time, so he had to rapidly chase the ball all the way to the wall. Mid-sprint, he not only managed to launch himself into the air to snag it (while hurtling face-first into said wall), but possessed both the coordination and wherewithal to throw directly to the cut-off man after the catch was made.

What happened next is the source of the worst kind of beer-drinking dismay among nostalgic old-timers. Braves runners Deion Sanders and Terry Pendleton crossed up, and Pendleton was called out for passing Sanders on the base path. Meanwhile, the ball sailed into first baseman John Olerud's glove, and he seamlessly threw to third baseman Kelly Gruber for the final out. Gruber speedily chased down Sanders and tagged him on the heel as Sanders dove for second base. The umpire, Bob Davidson, called Sanders safe, denying the team what everyone knew was a triple play. (And what would have been just the second triple play in World Series history.)

After all was said and done, that single catch captured my burgeoning baseball imagination like no other thing I had ever seen. It would have been enough that White sacrificially launched himself headlong into the abyss, but then he went on, impossibly, to get the ball into what was, Davidson be damned, indeed a triple play. Many have since compared the moment to Willie Mays's famed catch from Game One of the 1954 World Series, some even saying the 1990s version was more impressive than the original. Count no less an authority than Vin Scully among that group: "I saw Mays's catch. And this one, to me, was better."

Devon White, or "Devo," will always be remembered for that moment, but of course there was so much more to his sixteen-year career than just Game Three. Born Devon Whyte in Kingston, Jamaica, he immigrated to the U.S. with his family when he was nine; subsequent paperwork misspelled his name as "White." At the request of his children (his daughter is professional basketball player Davellyn LaRae Whyte), he legally changed his last name back to its original spelling in 2003, yet still signs autographs "Devon White."

Devo came to the Blue Jays from the Los Angeles Angels in 1990, and retired with the Milwaukee Brewers in 2001. He has three World Series rings and seven Gold Gloves, and was a three-time All-Star. In 2015, I watched as he threw out the first pitch at one of the Blue Jays' postseason games, and 50,000 people stood to honour him. He has said that people stop him all the time to talk about The Catch, and though he is gracious about how it figures into our formative baseball memories, it certainly doesn't define the player he was, or the person he is.

We come to love the players we do by the sheer force of randomness and circumstance. Sure, Devo was a great ballplayer—that point is indisputable—but the reason I fell in love with him that day, the reason I call him my favourite Blue Jay of all time, came to be via a confluence of moments and feelings that would be impossible to unravel. He astounded me at the exact moment I was old enough to be astounded, the exact moment I needed to be astounded, the exact moment I truly understood the physical feats necessary for the perfect execution of that play.

I was a thirteen-year-old girl looking for something to love, and he hurled himself at a wall beneath my feet, bringing an entire game and all of its history with him.

The thing about that barefoot moment in the outfield that I'd waited for since I watched The Catch in 1992? The hero himself was there in the moment I slipped my shoes off. About twenty feet away, Devo sat at a folding table signing autographs for eager children and nostalgic adults, his signature smile as wide and bright as I remembered it.

Standing there shoeless, I realized I didn't need to close my eyes to commune with the baseball gods—one of them was right there on the field with me.

"The reality is I never forget where I come from. Every day you bump into people complaining about life. When you see things like this, you have to thank God every day for being able to wake up and be healthy."

DAVID ORTIZ

on meeting his biggest fan, six-year-old Maverick, who was born with a heart defect

"Happiness is an attitude. We either make ourselves miserable, or joyous and peaceful; the amount of work is the same."

JASON GRILLI

on Twitter

"Our destiny's within our control."

JOSÉ BAUTISTA

"I'm ready to go out there and beat some folks, win some ball games, chest-bump with these guys, and eat some gummy bears. You know what I'm saying?"

COLBY RASMUS

WATCHING LIKE A GIRL

A few years ago, I was at a Blue Jays home game at the Rogers Centre when a kindly usher took it upon himself, unsolicited, to explain to me how many strikes make up an out, and how many balls are a walk. While I'm sure he had the best intentions at heart, the trouble with his instruction was that he assumed I needed it—I've been going to games for more than thirty years.

Men tend to make these assumptions, but like most female baseball fans I know, I actually have a specialized knowledge of the game that my male counterparts may not. For example, I know which sections of the ballpark are the safest for me to sit in, where I am least likely to be harassed or to overhear sexist, homophobic, or racist remarks from the male voices around me (at the Rogers Centre, 515, 204, and 113 are all good sections). I know that weekday evening games tend to be the most comfortable for women, that Sunday afternoons are generally calmer than Saturdays, and that Friday evenings are usually rowdy boozefests that should be avoided all together. I know that the centre-field porch on the 200 level—although equipped with a beautiful view—is generally out of the question if you're interested in avoiding spectators who are far too intoxicated to care about their fellow fans.

Most women I know simply want to have the same stadium experience that men enjoy, but they have to navigate baseball differently by necessity, as media messaging and an occasionally toxic ballpark environment consistently tell us this is a male space that we're being "allowed" to enter. In fact, I would say that I am a devoted fan of the game despite—and not because of—the culture that surrounds it.

According to a 2014 Nielsen study, women make up 35 per cent of sports fandom across North American professional sports leagues, and yet men hold an overwhelming majority of the power when it comes to creating mainstream sports culture—whether as a fan, or by being a sportswriter, on-air personality, or member of an MLB front office. Male athletes also dominate sports media coverage, leaving many female leagues with very little coverage at all. As a result, female sports fans are often left out of the conversation, and we find ourselves being told what we want and will enjoy, instead of being able to articulate it ourselves.

Though Major League Baseball wants to profit off its growing female fanbase, it would seem the powers that be still haven't found a way to include women in a way that isn't patronizing, idiotic, or downright offensive. Nowhere is the sad result of this rampant exclusion more apparent than in the ill-conceived initiatives that are designed to "cater" directly to us. While I'm sure they are dreamt up with the intention of being more inclusive, female-targeted events ("Girls' Night Out!") and merchandise ("Pink It and Shrink It!") have a tendency to rely on reductive preconceptions of what it means to be a woman and love this game. Walk into almost any ballpark's official store and you'll see a women's section littered with sequins, sparkles, and shades of pastel. The Texas Rangers offer a "Fields of Fashion" night to their female patrons, something that includes a Q&A with players' wives, a fashion show, wine tasting, and a Mother's Day celebration. (The connection between motherhood and female fandom is fierce and pervasive, best encapsulated by players donning MLB-enforced, pink-accented uniforms during the annual North American celebration of moms.)

In other misguided attempts to meet the needs of stereotypical femininity, female Atlanta Braves fans got a complimentary feather boa during their night out at Turner Field, while the Philadelphia Phillies marketed a Phillies Wives recipe book with healthy-cooking options, and a "Baseball 101 for Women" that assumes that only women, and never men, are confused by the nuances of the game. Sometimes it really feels like Major

League Baseball believes its female fans consist solely of baseball knowledge–impaired, wine-drinking moms dressed in pink.

A piece that I find myself referring back to when thinking about these issues is a July 2013 column in the *Globe and Mail*, titled "A new generation of baseball fans in Toronto are young, hip and cool." In it, the author offers a breakdown of the results of an in-stadium survey of 2012 Blue Jays game attendees conducted by Ipsos-Reid, and in doing so reinforces the condescending and hostile attitude that is the reason why I have to so carefully select my seats in the stadium. He attempts to explain an "astounding" 30 to 50 per cent jump in the attendance of women aged 18 to 34 at the Rogers Centre between 2010 and 2012 by lazily hypothesizing that these women aren't really baseball fans at all.

Through some rather biased quotation choices ("I'm not sure we're actually watching the game, to be clear . . . It's the best patio in the city, the best people-watching in the city"; "we can 'watch' the game—in quotations"), the column paints a singular portrait of a woman out for a night of drinking beer and gawking at boys. "Along with a number of other women interviewed for this story, she indicated the club's eye-appealing roster has enhanced her interest," it says of one subject. By cherry-picking comments and manufacturing conclusions, the writer does his part to contribute to a long-standing image problem that many female fans rail against.

While that article is from a few years ago, for me it's long epitomized how, to the media at large, baseball fans of the female persuasion tend to be seen as vapid, bored, and distracted. They're either dragged along by boyfriends or only there to party and pick up, whether for a ladies' night or a bachelorette party, all the while wearing their Hello Kitty accessories and Victoria's Secret Jays tees and drooling over Josh Donaldson. Women certainly can't be at the ballpark for any "real love" of the game, yet they do come in handy as the occasional pretty face for Sportsnet to zoom in on during a break in the action.

I in no way deny that these kinds of fans exist, nor do I think that they're a problem. The issue here lies in how both the media and Major League Baseball consistently portray a very limited and skewed depiction of women's relationship to sports, fostering all those pesky, mainstream assumptions that there's only one kind of female fan. This does real damage to the important project of attracting a new and diverse fanbase, a mission that not only makes good economic sense for MLB, but improves the overall experience for everyone.

The solution, it would seem, would be for Major League Baseball to find a happy medium between completely ignoring that women exist and speaking to them in patronizing and demeaning ways that make clear the league assumes they're all the same. ("The same" being a cardboard cut-out version of "femaleness" more suitable for prime-time sitcoms than the ballpark.)

If Major League Baseball is in any way invested in cultivating and profiting from its growing female audience, it would be wise to rethink how it markets the game to women, and to consider the role it plays in how its female fanbase is treated by mainstream sports media. I mean, why would you ever want to support, with your dollars or your love, a franchise that doesn't respect your knowledge, interest, or passion for it? That assumes you are stupid, but hopes you are pretty?

The idea that women don't really watch or understand the intricacies of sport sadly permeates a great deal of sports coverage. Writing for The Score, Ellen Etchingham astutely summed up our severely myopic view of female sports fandom in her takedown of *While the Men Watch*, CBC's abhorrent 2012 Stanley Cup Final hockey feed for women. Etchingham takes issue with the CBC's depiction of women as needing to have a separate, less in-depth conversation about the sport than men, and describes the stereotype of female viewers as follows: "Women don't understand sports. Women don't care about sports. If women watch sports, they only do so because a man pushes it on them. Women are interested in fashion, cleaning, shopping, and men."

Etchingham further articulates how offensive it is for female fans to have this heteronormative femininity constantly pushed on us by the media, as many use sports to actually escape that very thing. For her, hockey has been a haven, a break from strict societal norms. "For many of the so-called serious female fans, watching the game is one of the best social avenues for meeting people and hanging out in a relatively ungendered way," she explains. "Being into sports allows us to be guys, not in the sense of men, but in the sense of participants in a laid-back, friendly, easygoing social milieu that doesn't feel defined by gender lines. Many female fans explicitly resist the category 'female fans,' because for us part of what is great about being a fan is the sense that female or male doesn't matter so much."

When I expressed on social media my disdain for that *Globe and Mail* article's flawed take, I brattily retitled the piece: "Why women go to baseball games, by a male sports journalist." Several female fans got in touch to share my sentiment: women who attend games with scorecards in hand, who have encyclopedic knowledge of players, stats, and history, who have romantic ideals about the game's meaning and thc narrative it provides them. These are women who attend (and spend) with the knowledge that the system excludes and disrespects them, yet they try to carve out a space for themselves anyway. When it is so difficult for them to participate, when they have to work so much harder to be included, why would anyone ever doubt how much they love it?

What bothers me about that piece, and those like it, is how it reinforces the antagonistic attitude many male fans have about women being in "their" ballpark—as if a bunch of girls chatting about wedding plans instead of paying attention to the action is more off-putting than "real fans" yelling homophobic slurs and harassing the people around them. It points to an ingrained belief that women don't belong, which is exacerbated by an appalling gender imbalance in terms of who is "allowed" to talk publicly about "Dad's game."

Unlike other journalistic fields, sports reporting, in all its forms, has mysteriously remained immune to open discussions about gender parity. So many mastheads and sports desks remain dominated by male voices and faces, with nary a criticism when compared to other increasingly diverse media categories. It's as if we've collectively accepted that sports is a man's domain, and so men alone should speak on it. With the success of writers like Etchingham at The Score, Sarah Spain at espnW, Kristina Rutherford at Sportsnet, and Katie Baker at The Ringer, and editors like Caitlin Kelly at Vice Sports, things are definitely changing—but it's hard to deny that women have traditionally been offered very few roles in North American professional sports culture, most of which amount to "look pretty and say little."

There are, however, reasons to be optimistic about the future, beyond subtle shifts in sports media mastheads. In September 2016, the L.A. Dodgers hosted a "Take Your Daughter to a Game" day at Dodger Stadium. While this empowering initiative is a big leap forward for Major League Baseball, it's worth noting that the impetus for the event was a partnership with Fox television's *Pitch*, a prime-time drama about a female pitcher who makes it to the big leagues. What was indeed buoying about the marketing for the event was that, beyond catering to daughters, it didn't feature any noticeable gender signifiers (participants received a personalized trading card and were invited to see a screening of the show prior to its premiere date). It was a step forward, even if it was one prompted by the promotion of a feminist-minded television show and not necessarily by MLB's own vested interest.

The people behind *Pitch* may have understood they were targeting a large and under-served female audience, but the mainstream media still struggled with the concept. The same month Dodgers fans were bringing their daughters to a game at *Pitch*'s invitation, the *New York Times* ran a review of the show, tweeting, "How will *Pitch* cater to the hard-core baseball fan expecting authenticity while still appealing to women?" The inherent presupposition that women can't be hardcore baseball fans sparked a trending hashtag on Twitter, #ThisIsWhatABaseballFanLooksLike, where female fans posted pictures of themselves dressed in their beloved team's gear, hanging out with their female friends and daughters at the ballpark. It was hard, grassroots evidence that baseball isn't simply a place for men—women too have a desire to be there.

More importantly, we deserve to be.

I certainly don't deny that some people go to games simply to have a drink or two and people-watch, and I don't deny that some of those people are women (nor do I think there's anything wrong with that). What is important here is to recognize and call out the emphasis we put on supposed female ignorance, disinterest, and frivolity when we talk about female baseball fandom, and the way we exclude women from the larger dialogue as a consequence. Every fan's personal experience of the game is different, regardless of gender, and the stereotypes we reinforce only limit and harm the overall community. It surely couldn't have been hard for a reporter to find a quotable female fan who could talk complex stats, or who had more than a passing interest in the game, instead of focusing solely on attendees who confirmed the expectations of the status quo.

Men go to the ballpark with an assumed knowledge and interest, whereas women need to constantly demonstrate how much they know and care. A radically different take on that Ipsos-Reid survey is that maybe, despite the hostility female fans encounter every time we go to the ballpark or read the sports pages, we're making a bold attempt to secure a spot for ourselves in a culture that has omitted us. Despite what sports culture may believe, many women deeply love what has long been considered a man's game, and the time is overdue for the gatekeepers of fandom to accept, support, and welcome this growing audience, and for sports media to report on them in a non-biased way.

In Etchingham's brilliant words, "Don't tell me you respect serious female fans. If you did, you'd have found some."

AND THE BAND PLAYED ON

October 15, 2015

The game of baseball is usually made up of long pauses punctuated by tiny miracles. It's often ridiculed for the clock-less way it drags on toward infinity, a team sport that actually reads more like an anthology of small solo victories.

A pitcher on fire, serious and stoic while counting up his Ks. A centre fielder with an incredible home run–stealing catch. And of course a storied slugger, hurling that tiny white ball over a wall 400 feet away. Each action is carried out by a single man, and most actions are much less emotionally and physically aggressive than those of other professional athletes.

But the "win or go home" Game Five of the American League Division Series matchup between the Toronto Blue Jays and the Texas Rangers felt like a decidedly different affair. It was the kind of game that turns non-believers of the collectively induced magic of baseball into teary-eyed converts. It was the kind of game we'll tell our bored children and grandchildren about years from now, a well-worn badge of pride if we're able to say we were there.

That already historic fifty-three-minute seventh inning, long enough that you could have watched an entire episode of prime-time dramatic television, felt like it had a momentum driven entirely by the team's and the fans' shared feelings. Disappointment, frustration, misery, rage, and then, finally, an elation like no other in sports. It was an Italian opera. A Shakespearean play. A truly ensemble effort. Many a seasoned baseball writer has said they have seen no game like it, and likely never will again. This is exactly the game you refer to when people say that baseball is boring, so thoroughly does it turn their claim to lie.

I was at yesterday's game, carefully dressed in the exact same clothes I wore during the final home game of the regular season—a T-shirt and cap made lucky because Josh Donaldson hit a walk-off home run, was promptly stripped of his jersey, and then ceremonially soaked in Powerade. I'll admit here that I haven't been handling the playoffs well. At the beginning of this ALDS, I suffered through the Jays' devastating Game One and Two losses—the stress, and the stress hangovers from each making me a basket case, more apt to cry over baseball feelings than usual.

The Jays had managed comfortable wins in Games Three and Four, but by yesterday, with the team back at home for the final contest, my faith was considerably shaken. I'm ashamed to admit there was a small part of me that had already resigned myself to a loss—a thing we've been trained to do for decades as Toronto sports fans. (We can't be blamed for our defence mechanisms.) Naturally, the do-or-die nature of Game Five was an inevitable torture chamber for the sports-sensitive, and I found myself putting my head between my knees and practising deep-breathing exercises to make it through. (Hilarious, given I often say a visit to the ballpark is a great way to relieve stress.)

The seventh inning was the worst of it, best described by SB Nation's Grant Brisbee: "There will never be an inning like this again. Send the whole thing to Cooperstown and bury it." The bulk of the drama commenced when—with the score tied at two, a runner on third, and two outs—Jays catcher Russell Martin's return throw to the mound hit Ranger Shin-Soo Choo's bat and created a crazy situation where Rougned Odor was allowed to score. Multiple arduous umpire and manager conferences commenced on the call, the lengthy break allowing for a fierce buzzing anxiety to rise in an already temperamental Rogers Centre.

There was no way we were willing to lose this way; no way we were willing to go down on a rarely implemented unintentional interference rule that seemed unjust.

Trash started to rain down on the field. Full beer cans were thrown, with one spraying beer on an unwitting baby. People aggressively chanted "bullshit," and everyone looked ready to burn the whole place down. Players peeked out of the dugout to discourage fans from throwing things. Friends started texting me, asking if I was safe at my seat. Eventually I retreated to the bathroom, only to find angry people smoking.

The Rangers led 3–2 as we went into the bottom of the seventh, with the Jays playing under protest.

Then came an unexpected and welcome downpour of Texas errors. Russell Martin got on base. Kevin Pillar got on base. Quick-footed Dalton Pompey pinch-ran for Martin and advanced on another error, only to end up out at home on a Ben Revere hit. Josh Donaldson appeared at the plate like the saviour he is, tying everything up by knocking out a single that sent Pillar home and answered my literal, pleading call of "Fix this, Josh." 3–3. In terms of being in a position to win, "we" were right back where we started before the very ugly inning began.

And then José Bautista did the most José Bautista thing imaginable. I've watched the moment easily a dozen times since it happened, and it never loses its intensity or its poetry. The undisputed king of the "fuck you" home run, Toronto's all-star Silver Slugger got his ultimate, well-deserved revenge with a miraculous three-run blast. (I'm tearing up again just thinking about it.) The incredulous, in-your-face bat flip that followed could easily be the most justified showboating in the history of baseball. 6–3. Make a bronze statue of that man immediately.

From there we saw even more bench-clearing spats and fan misbehaviour, with the security and police officers on hand certainly earning their paycheques. By the time twenty-year-old closing pitcher Roberto Osuna came in to shut the whole preposterous affair down, we were all wondering what had actually happened over the past four hours. What was clear was that the Jays had gained the upper hand in the most dramatic way possible, and with that last strikeout (punctuated by Osuna making his signature lengthy sign of the cross), the delirious celebration rivalled the game itself in terms of emotional impact.

Generally sombre knuckleballer R.A. Dickey was exuberant, enthusiastically high-fiving a long line of fans in the front row. He passed one a bottle of champagne, took others' phones and snapped pictures, and at one point kissed a vintage SkyDome children's stuffed turtle named "Domer." He patted the butts of police officers, and then threw himself into the crowd for a warm collective embrace. Catcher Dioner Navarro somehow managed to score a police officer's hat and wore it authoritatively while sucking on a cigar. Comeback kid Marcus Stroman jumped up and onto his mentor, Mark "Papa" Buehrle, in what might be one of the greatest baseball hugs of all time.

Of Bautista's home run, Josh Donaldson said, "This guy is my hero."

After the final out last night, I made my way through the jubilant crowds and went home to rewatch the game from the seventh inning onward. Seeing it on screen made the whole thing feel almost fake, like a heartstring-tugging movie, as if someone had scripted it for maximum emotional impact. It was simultaneously so unlike baseball, and also exactly the baseball I love the most—harrowing, excruciating, hopeful, and ultimately triumphant.

When it comes to sports, Toronto is a city that doesn't really know how to win, and these Blue Jays keep forcing us to understand that it's possible. This team, with all its storybook individual victories, actually feels more cohesive than any other I've ever witnessed, and has brought this city together in a way I could never have conceived.

THANK YOU, ALISON GORDON

I never had a chance to meet groundbreaking Canadian sportswriter Alison Gordon, but I've been thinking a lot about her over the past few years.

I thought about her when I started writing about baseball, consumed by the nagging false doubt that I had "no right" to do so. I thought about her during my first baseball scrum, as I nervously thrust my tape recorder toward Blue Jays outfielder José Bautista while being bounced around by a throng of male reporters. I thought about her when I received a defensive, expletive-filled email (nine F-words, and one S-word) from a sports-event organizer after I publicly suggested he consider more diversity on his all-white, all-male panel.

I think about Gordon whenever I look at the home-page lineup of Sportsnet's "Insiders," mostly white male faces reporting on subject matter that has a significant female audience. I think about her when I'm patronizingly marketed sparkly pink baseball merchandise and baseball-themed nail polish, or forced to watch an all-female dance troupe perform in short skirts for the crowd at the Rogers Centre. I think about her whenever it feels too hard, too tiring, or too hopeless to be a part of the sports conversation—to endure the sexism it breeds. I then remind myself that Gordon weathered so much more, so much worse, and did it, by all reports, with a smile on her face.

Gordon died unexpectedly on February 12, 2015, at the age of seventy-two, after surgery for a lung condition. She was beloved and revered by everyone who knew her, and by many who didn't. When I tentatively started writing about baseball, some of her friends said to me, "Have you met Alison Gordon yet? You have to meet Alison." She was the first female American League beat writer, and given how challenging it is to be a female sportswriter even today, that was no small feat more than thirty years ago.

Born in New York, Gordon spent her childhood in places like Tokyo, Cairo, and Rome, because her Canadian father worked for the UN. She attended Queen's University in Kingston, Ontario, but left before she completed her degree, going on to work for Pierre Elliott Trudeau, and also to sit at the foot of John and Yoko's bed at their Montreal bed-in for peace. Gordon's sportswriting career really took off in 1979, when the *Toronto Star* assigned her the daunting (and male-dominated) task of covering the fledgling Toronto Blue Jays. By all accounts—including her own—she was thick-skinned and relentless in the face of myriad forms of abuse, from people (i.e., men) either perplexed by her presence or offended by her "audacity" in setting foot in an all-boys' club. Her Baseball Writers' Association of America card—the first ever issued to a woman—famously read "Mr. Alison Gordon," simply because there was no option for anything else.

"I didn't start the job with any stirring sense of historic destiny," Gordon wrote in her 1984 essay collection, *Foul Balls: Five Years in the American League*:

> I was no brave pioneer on feminism's cutting edge. I was just another scared rookie on the way to my first spring training, playing a new game at which I would have to make up the rules. I wasn't only new to baseball, I was new to newspapers, and there were more than several people waiting for me to fall on my face.

Alison Gordon deeply loved baseball and its human side until the day she died. She spent five years with the Jays, enduring protests against letting a woman into the locker room "on religious grounds," verbal objections that the clubhouse should be maintained as a man's domain, and all the expected offensive remarks and obscene gestures. There were attempts to intimidate and insult her; sometimes the fact she was a woman got more attention than the game itself. After her first season she received a letter that read, "Madam—I see where you don't seem to mind male nudity in athletes shower rooms at sports arenas. Well, neither would any whore." But still Gordon found the will to go to work and do her job well for four more seasons. In 1979 she won a National Newspaper Award for her sportswriting, and in 1984 she published *Foul Balls*, a book that unabashedly recounts the trials of being a lone woman in an aggressively male arena.

Being off the beat didn't mean that she abandoned baseball writing; instead she used her experience as fodder for five popular baseball mystery novels, the central character a crime-solving sports reporter. She also had musical interests: for the decade before her death, the Toronto rock band 3 Chord Johnny rehearsed in her basement, a regular Wednesday evening get-together that, according to members, was as much about "the hang" as it was about the music. Gordon presided over the kitchen table they congregated at, usually offering her superb guacamole.

"Alison was a feisty, funny, smart, sometimes testy, always thoughtful woman," says band member, friend, and writer David Hayes. "Her sense of humour could fairly be called 'salty,' I'd say. I doubt I even scratched the surface of knowing everything about the incredible experiences she had throughout her life."

It would seem Gordon's saltiness and sense of humour served her well in enduring the jabs of being a woman in sports media. It's been more than three decades since she bravely made her mark, and though there's been a great deal of progress over that time, pervasive sexism in the sports world certainly still exists. What that environment does to a writer's psyche, and how it sullies the thing you love, is hard to explain to someone who hasn't endured it—and what's worse is there aren't a lot of women who feel safe publicly discussing it. Talking about the toxicity can put their coveted jobs at risk, and can lead to ejection from the community. In my short time writing about baseball, I've heard women speak in public about how "supportive and professional" colleagues and players are, and then privately tell sinister stories. I've been in conversations with young women breaking into sports media who have a jaw-droppingly long and appalling list of gender-based grievances. The harassment is anything from dick jokes to ass-grabbing, from being invited by a player back to his hotel to insults such as this personal favourite: "Do you even like sports?" With every snide comment and instance of bad male behaviour, women are either told to "take a joke" or accused of not being able to hack it.

One of the most important ways to create a better, more comfortable place for women in sports is to have more of them—their voices and their ideas—in the media. Whether they know it or not, the women who endure sports' sexist trials are shifting things toward something better, more robust, and more inclusive for everyone. Not only are they battling daily to do and talk about what they love, they're creating a safer and more welcoming atmosphere for the women who come after them, just like Gordon did in 1979. It's an arduous but necessary process, applying not only to beat writers or TV personalities, but also to bloggers, tweeters, and any women who assert their fandom and say, "We're allowed to be here."

And despite the slow evolution, it's working.

About a week before Gordon died, my boss at the time walked into my office and casually handed me her tattered hardcover copy of *Foul Balls*. She knew of my rabid love of baseball, and asked if I'd ever met her trailblazing friend. I told her I hadn't, but said I'd love the chance to thank Gordon for everything she'd done. My boss promised to set up a meeting. I'll never get that chance to express my gratitude to Gordon in person now, but I can help continue the work that she started. She provided a model for carving out a vital space for women in sports, and relentlessly asserted that we deserve to be here, and we deserve better. Even when it gets hard, hopeless, and daunting, I can wake up the next day and do it again, because that's what Gordon would have done. That's what Gordon did.

PLAYING THE LONG GAME

On April 10, 2015, the Boston Red Sox beat the New York Yankees, 6–5, in what turned out to be the longest game in the former's franchise history. Clocking in at an absurd six hours and forty-nine minutes, the nineteen-inning marathon included a sixteen-minute power outage that temporarily put out a section of lights at Yankee Stadium. According to the *New York Times*, when the Red Sox finally turned the game-ending double play at 2:13 a.m., "Yankee Stadium was empty enough to hear their celebratory shouts as players and coaches emptied out of the dugout."

It's an interesting bit of irony that this excruciating slog of a game was played by Boston. Outspoken Sox slugger David Ortiz (who hit a home run in the sixteenth) has been a vocal opponent of Major League Baseball's 2015-instituted pace-of-play rules, all designed to quicken a famously slow pastime. When asked at a press conference what he thought of a rule that requires batters to keep a foot in the box during an entire at-bat, he said: "I call that bullshit... It's not like you go to the plate with an empty mind... When I come out I'm thinking what is this guy going to try to do to me next? I'm not walking around because there's cameras all over the place and I want my buddies back home to see me."

It turns out Ortiz is not alone in his pace-of-play protest and belief in the meditative nature of the game. In an informal 2015 ESPN poll of 117 major-league players, 60 per cent said they didn't think the game was too slow, and an overwhelming 78 per cent said they disliked the idea of a pitch clock. Diehard devotees often assert that in a world that demands we constantly be on schedule, the lack of a clock is part of baseball's dawdling charm—that it's a gift not to be able to make solid, immovable plans at the end of nine innings. "Uh, it's not like a Broadway musical where it ends with a big Hawaiian number," says Red Sox fanatic Ben Wrightman in the 2005 film *Fever Pitch*, when his uninitiated, workaholic girlfriend asks what time the game is over.

Yet, despite the objections of both players and "more traditional" fans, speeding up the game has been a high priority for Major League Baseball since August 2014, when owners elected Rob Manfred the tenth commissioner of baseball. Fear of the game's aging fan demographic—the average age is mid-fifties, considerably older than NFL and NBA watchers—and falling television ratings are the league's impetus for change. Major League

Baseball has formed a special committee to create, examine, and enforce rules that promise to shave time off the average game-length of three hours. Hitters who don't fall in line with batter's box requirements, for example, will first face warnings, and then an escalating series of fines that top out at $500 per infraction. "I might run out of money," Ortiz said. (The Red Sox paid him $16 million during the 2015 season.)

Thanks to Manfred, the insidious red glow of a timer is now present in stadiums, with countdowns indicating how long breaks between each half-inning should last. Pitchers are required to throw their last warm-up pitch with thirty seconds remaining, and batters should be in the box by twenty.

Then there's the overwhelmingly loathed twenty-second pitch clock that has already been implemented at Double-A and Triple-A levels, training prospects to get used to its ominous presence before it is instituted MLB-wide in the future. (As of May 1, 2015, a Double-A or Triple-A umpire is able to call a ball if the clock reaches zero before the pitcher throws.) Other agenda items that have been under committee consideration? Limiting the number of relievers that a team can use during a game, and reducing the number of warm-up throws from those relief pitchers. The strategy is to slowly but surely encourage players to change their habits, and, by extension, quicken the general rhythm of the game.

Early reports say the league's lofty plan is working, at least in its mission to tighten things up—it's still unclear whether it will amount to anything dollars-wise. Though certainly a meagre sample, the first thirty-five games of 2015 saw nine-inning contests last an average two hours and fifty-two minutes, down ten minutes through the same number the previous year.

Major League Baseball has invested a great deal of time, energy, talk, and money into saving all its potential new fans an entire ten minutes they will not have to spend in the ballpark or on their couches. They've made a statement that they're serious about change, with a promise that more minutes will be shaved off in the future.

Does this mean all of baseball's non-fans—time-sensitive folks, every last one—have begun flocking to parks in droves? Does it mean these mythical younger viewers, with their (alleged) impatience and limited attention spans, are suddenly seeing the game's newfound briskness and climbing on board? Entirely unlikely. In fact, I would assert that the thing that Major League Baseball consistently misses is that its audience problem is less about how long the game experience lasts, and more about who is allowed to be a part of it.

It's true that the game is far too mired in outdated tradition, but it's the culture that's regressive, not the clock. On April 6, 2015, David Price became the first black pitcher to start Opening Day for the Detroit Tigers in forty-seven years. That year, Major League Baseball had just one black manager, the Seattle Mariners' Lloyd McClendon. All ten baseball commissioners in history, from Kenesaw Mountain Landis (1920–1944) to Manfred (2015–present), have been white men.

Meanwhile, Major League Baseball is taking its sweet time in getting rid of the Cleveland Indians' "Chief Wahoo," arguably the most racist mascot in all of professional sports. There are currently no out gay major-league ballplayers, and only around half of the league's thirty teams have ever hosted an LGBT Pride Night. Baseball has successfully alienated the mentally ill with its inability to properly deal with concussion-related injuries, has let down domestic violence and rape survivors with its prior poor record of reprimanding offenders, and with the Los Angeles Angels' punishment and rejection of Josh Hamilton it has abandoned those who struggle with addiction. Most efforts to make women feel welcome at the ballpark are limited to pink-washed breast cancer awareness, a "Girls' Night Out," and Mother's Day events.

And if we're talking about lofty plans for change, what if MLB's gatekeepers consciously valued diversity in the media they give access to? What if they further denied access to those who have made a habit of broadcasting or printing sexist, racist, and homophobic comments?

In March 2015, Oakland Athletics pitcher Sean Doolittle and his partner, Eireann Dolan, made a public offer to purchase tickets from season ticket holders who expressed "discomfort" over the team's announcement of its first Pride Night. The offer was to buy any unwanted tickets to the upcoming June 17 game at face value, with a plan to fill the stadium by donating the seats to Our Space, a Bay Area program for LGBT youth. None of the homophobic fans took the bait, so Dolan instead raised money for members of Our Space to attend, with a commitment from Dolan and Doolittle to match donations up to $3,000. (Any money not used for ticket purchases was divided between Our Space, AIDS Project East Bay, and Frameline, a distributor of award-winning LGBT films and videos.)

Dolan and Doolittle's non-MLB-affiliated fundraising efforts got press outside the narrow field of baseball reporting, and garnered a great deal of attention from those who have only a fleeting interest in the game. The widespread reception has been: "I don't care about baseball, but this is great." It's actions like theirs—not Manfred's—that make the game relevant, and encourage fandom from those who've long seen it as exclusionary and stuck in the past.

On that historic Friday night in April 2015, when the Red Sox finally beat the Yankees after six hours and forty-nine minutes, baseball asserted that it will take all the time that it needs, thank you very much. While it's certain that the league must dramatically evolve to attract new audiences, all this attention on speeding things up feels like a case of misplaced resources and energy. Manfred's first priority to attract a new generation of fans to their old man's game is necessary, but his methods so far are likely both futile and fruitless. The message to Major League Baseball should be clear: let's open doors by working on the things we can—and should—change.

Anything else, as Ortiz would put it, is bullshit.

"You've got to keep your head up and searching for answers and keep grinding it out, and know there are many seasons within a season."

R.A. DICKEY

"I choose to see light still. It's just a matter of, when something bad goes on, you don't fall into that trap of getting sucked in real fast. It's going to happen every day."

PAUL MOLITOR

on the Twins' dismal 2016 record

"We are never scared. We still have very important games to come. We want to stay focused. No thinking. Just swing. Just throw. Just catch. Don't think, everybody. Just win."

MUNENORI KAWASAKI

"You tip your hat and move on."

MARCO ESTRADA

on giving up a run during a June 2016 no-hit bid

THE YEAR IN COMING CLOSE

I'm not sure exactly when I developed the habit, but at some point in my baseball-watching career I started wagering on games.

I don't mean in the traditional gambling sense. Instead, I would tell myself that if there was a victorious baseball outcome, it would have implications in my day-to-day life. For example, if José Bautista hits during this bases-loaded-tied-in-extras game, it means the universe will give me that much-needed raise I've been hoping for. If Marcus Stroman pitches that one last strikeout, that health issue I've been worrying about will turn out to be nothing. If Josh Donaldson produces a walk-off home run in the ninth inning of the last home game of the season, everything will work out just fine.

I would sit in my Rogers Centre seat and suspend my disbelief, childishly thinking that the baseball gods would take time out of their busy schedules to send personalized messages my way. Rational and even cynical in my non-baseball life, I'd treat a regular-season game like it was some sort of psychic divining rod dictating my fate. This odd practice soon evolved into involuntary impulse—a wager would suddenly pop into my head at any given pivotal moment during the game, and whatever happened at the plate would become loaded with meaning.

As a long-suffering Blue Jays fan, I made these tiny and perhaps foolish wagers over years and years of inconsequential games. I never actually tracked the accuracy of the baseball gods on their imaginary calls, but that always felt kind of beside the point. I was likely doing it for a harmless jolt of magic, a flirtation with the divine for someone without much investment in any higher power otherwise. It was a prayer of sorts. But when the 2015 season rolled around, everything became so much more weighted, every tiny moment so much more meaningful.

The month that Blue Jays pitchers and catchers reported to spring training marked the first anniversary of my husband and me trying to have a baby. Given that my thirty-sixth birthday fell on Opening Day, and all those previous months of bouncing between fingers-crossed hope and total disappointment, the baseball season coincided exactly with a medically dictated need to "take the issue seriously."

For those unaware, taking the inability to get pregnant seriously means invasive, anxiety-inducing tests and a barrage of insensitive questions from doctors. It means acupuncture, supplements, injections, and restrictive diets. It means arduous cycle-tracking, daily temperature-taking, clunky and expensive ovulation kits, and difficult emotional and monetary decisions about treatment and procedures. More embarrassingly, it means an ugly low-level resentment for every single pregnancy announcement and birth you're privy to. It means earnest counselling and inevitable public weeping. And for me it meant a final, painful diagnosis of "unexplained infertility"—a frustrating combination of words that together mean something is wrong, but no one has any idea how to fix it.

All of this also meant that baseball, the one place I had always gone to for solace in the face of painful circumstances, became ever the more vital. It didn't take long for me to realize that infertility is a taboo subject, something people either feel deeply uncomfortable addressing or are ill-equipped to talk about. Attempts to reach out to others about what I was feeling were often met with embarrassment, ignorance, or an entirely useless chorus of "just relax and it'll happen."

Baseball was a perhaps frivolous little diversion that kindly assuaged the silence and loneliness of grappling with my failure to conceive, but it was also my best treatment option. Despite how isolated and ashamed I felt because of what was quietly happening to me, despite feeling like I wasn't allowed to talk about it, even to the people I was closest to, I could go to a Sunday afternoon game, take in nine innings and a few beers, and feel decidedly less alone.

Lucky for me, the 2015 Toronto Blue Jays did an excellent job of distracting me from the inevitable abyss of "what ifs?" and "when?" with 173 home and away games over seven months. The team's increasing success blotted out my more fatalistic thoughts and emotions about infertility, and consistently gave me something to look forward to and celebrate when things felt truly dire. When I made the very difficult decision to quit my full-time job in the interest of reducing the stress that everyone kept citing as a problem, watching and writing about baseball gracefully filled my days, and silenced the nagging worry that I would never become a mother.

When the dog days of summer hit, the Blue Jays looked like genuine postseason contenders for the first time in decades. After taking a ballpark road trip to California in late July—one where I watched the Jays win a three-game series against the Oakland A's—I maintained my immovable faith and kept a keen eye on that arduous cycle-tracking. I returned to Toronto to watch a newly signed David Price magnificently debut at Rogers Centre with the knowledge that I was, after seventeen months of trying, finally late. A couple of days late turned into a couple of weeks late, and I couldn't help but selfishly think the baseball gods were rewarding me for my devotion.

And then, when I had a very early miscarriage in mid-August, the overwhelming feeling of personal failure was soothed by the team's sudden surge of success and all the public joy that surrounded it. It was the Jays, after all, who had taught me to get up again after setbacks and disappointments. It was the Jays who had taught me there'd always be another game.

Given my past history of making wagers, it was unavoidable I'd make the big one when the fall playoff buzz began. As I watched our boys of summer drench each other in bottles of Bud after taking the American League East, I suddenly thought, *If the Blue Jays win the World Series, I'll have a baby.*

I immediately hated myself for thinking it.

It may seem ridiculous to say so, but the game of baseball and all its clichés are much like dealing with infertility in the long term. There's a great deal of "maybe next time" that you tell yourself in the face of predictable, routine failure. The abundance of games, the lack of a running clock, the stats on success, the way you get up tomorrow and try again after brushing off another devastating defeat—all of that feels familiar to those determined to conceive in the face of repeated negative outcomes. After all, it's a long season. You've got so much time. You say "no big deal," and "I'm okay, just disappointed," and you move forward and try again. You know it's better and healthier not to stress or wallow. Never focus on yesterday's loss lest it derail you from seeing the potential of the future.

The October 2015 Blue Jays were a master class in bouncing back from setback. Putting on your Josh Donaldson jersey and attending those home games was like a training ground in resilience. Game Five of the American League Division Series against the Texas Rangers, with its fifty-three-minute seventh inning and now-mythical Bautista blast, was nothing less than an orgy of hope. Even in the more absurdly disappointing moments, like a demoralizing 14–2 blowout during the American League Championship Series that made Cliff Pennington the first position player in major-league history to pitch a playoff game, there was a certain levity to the letdown: Dioner Navarro laughed and clapped from the dugout as if there was always a tomorrow to turn things around. With all the stress, all the burying our faces in our hands and praying we could do it, there was a reigning, city-wide belief that was entirely glorious.

The sweet-faced counsellor the clinic assigned to me told me that part of the reason infertility is so emotionally harrowing is because we're falsely trained our whole lives to think that anything can be accomplished via hard work. If you want something bad enough, they say, it can be yours as long as you are willing to put in the time and make the necessary sacrifices to get it. But the truth is that sometimes life is simply nothing more than unfair, and no amount of effort or wanting or wishing for something will ever make it happen. Even though you're always going to cling to the smallest sliver of faith, even though you know how much you deserve it, you have to get comfortable with the fact that maybe something you want so badly will never be yours.

The final game of the Blue Jays' 2015 bid to get to the World Series—a best-avoided memory now—was rife with the most desperate kind of faith. The evening the Jays faced the Royals in Kansas City for Game Six of the ALCS, I was in a bar in Toronto and the mood was blistering, electric: every person in the room was connected in their firm belief that wanting it more, deserving it more, would dictate the final outcome. José Bautista was, as always, heroic, driving in three runs with a pair of homers, including a two-run shot that tied it up when the Jays were down to their dismal last five outs. When a forty-five-minute rain delay hit in the eighth inning, we all sang Drake's "Know Yourself" in unison, and drunkenly reminded ourselves it's never over until it's over.

And then Josh Donaldson grounded out to third, and it was over.

I'd been trying to get pregnant for nineteen months and twenty-three days.

—

I've often said that maybe those who have deeply emotional and perhaps even excessive reactions to sports are those who have difficulty expressing their feelings about other issues in their lives. When I hysterically wept in the back of a cab after the Jays lost their final shot, it was of course because I really wanted them to win, but it was also because I didn't know how to be upset about not being able to have a baby. I didn't know how to express my feelings about my early miscarriage, and I didn't know how to properly grieve something I never even knew. So instead I cried about a bunch of men not getting rings. It felt so much easier to weep for them than to look at my own complicated misery head-on.

It's strange to be so sad about not getting a thing you didn't even really think about having before. When you come so close and lose it, the aftermath tends to be a period of regret instead of a celebration of all the otherwise miraculous achievements behind you. In some ways we got greedy. We thought the feeling that we deserved something was enough to make it happen, and in doing so we forgot to applaud how far we'd come.

I really needed the Blue Jays to win the 2015 World Series. But maybe, according to the baseball gods, I needed them not to win a little bit more. Maybe it was more important that I abandon my big wager and come to terms with the fact that sometimes things are simply unjust, and we can't get what we want, and that it can be okay—even beautiful—regardless.

Maybe I needed to focus on what baseball has always taught me: it's a long season of many games, and there's always next year.

IT'S OKAY TO HAVE THE HOTS FOR BASEBALL PLAYERS: A MANIFESTO

Over the past few years, as my baseball fandom spiked to near-ridiculous levels, I found myself using a stock phrase when discussing my favourite players. "It's not a sex thing," I'd say when extolling the virtues of Justin Verlander or Buster Posey or Clayton Kershaw. For whatever reason, it was important to me that people (namely men) knew I was a thoroughly committed and unemotional devotee of the sport: someone not to be dismissed as a mere fangirl lusting after butts in belted baseball pants.

Female sports fans will know what I'm talking about—the nagging impulse to reassure others that you're not there for the obviously aesthetically pleasing on-field show.

A solely romantic appreciation for male athletes is certainly one of the more common accusations levied against ladies who like sports; it's a way to dismiss women's interest and knowledge as lesser than that of our male counterparts. In a culture where female voices are so often excluded—a quick glance at any roster of mainstream sportswriters and personalities bears this out—the perceived sin of physical attraction to the players is another reason to keep the "Members Only" sign up at the boys' club.

"As I started heading to more ballgames, I found random male strangers perfectly willing to point out that there was no way I could really know the game, and that any player whose name was on a jersey I might have been wearing was only someone I thought was hot," says K., a thirty-seven-year-old Blue Jays fan. "I tried my best to try to change their minds about it, but it was generally met with verbal pats on the head."

Being hot for players has long been a no-no for "serious" female fans, one that's ingrained in us from the age when crushes first start to blossom. (The same goes for male fans as well, obviously, but rampant homophobia in sports is another essay entirely.) Mabel, also a thirty-seven-year-old Jays fan, remembers feeling judged for her desires as soon as she was old enough to have them. "The timing of when people started wondering why I liked sports roughly coincided with young adulthood," she says. "Like, it's cute and okay for a thirteen-year-old to adore John Olerud. But a seventeen-year-old doing the same is wrong, as she's a woman, or close to."

While the expression and service of male heterosexual lust is one of our more pervasive, culturally permissible pastimes, female longing is policed well beyond sports fandom. It's viewed as everything from dismissible (think boy bands) to dangerous (slut-shaming). Women who want after male athletes wind up being labelled as jersey chasers or gold-diggers, or significantly (and predictably) worse.

Female sports fans in general are treated like a stock list of stereotypes: served up infantilizing pink, sequined baby tees and given institutionalized opportunities to "better understand" the game, invited to wine-soaked MLB-sponsored ladies' nights, or marketed Victoria's Secret gear emblazoned with "Let's kiss for the kiss cam!"

Further, it seems that sports culture can't reconcile female desire with knowledge, so if you're admiring the finer points of Josh Donaldson's unstoppable swagger—his "liquid hot sexual gold," as certain aficionados have been known to call it—you can't possibly understand the mechanics of his MVP-worthy work at third base. Logic would dictate that I can find him stunning and still understand how the game works, and even be an expert on it. Yet, for whatever reason, acknowledging that I notice how pretty he is somehow becomes a shameful admission. I am forever a guest in a man's house, and am expected to watch what I say and police what I feel accordingly.

Quite frankly, I've grown tired of pretending that Bryce Harper isn't a scorchingly beautiful specimen of masculinity. I've become exhausted denying that Buster

Posey has the most adorable, angelic boy-band face I've seen since perusing *Tiger Beat* as a teenage girl. I'm weary from saying that Justin Verlander's pants appear "uncomfortable," or that Matt Kemp looks "like an athlete." I've actually come to think that every time I deny my inevitable attraction to players—I'm only human, and you know what Matt Kemp looks like—I'm supporting that terrible notion that real fans don't have crushes, or that crushes hysterically cancel out all other considerations, or that women should simply shut up about how they feel if they want to watch the game with everyone else. A more cynical observer might even wonder if the cultural insistence that female fans adhere to this gag rule has more to do with not wanting to undermine the masculinity of the historically male fanbase than with any real concern about "respecting the game."

Other fans share my overall disdain for the way the female gaze is dismissed and derided in sports culture. Leesa let me know that she loves Josh Hamilton's batting bounce and beard, and that her favourite thighs in baseball (Leesa loves baseball thighs) belong to Mike Trout. For a long time, though, she kept those feelings to herself. "I learned very quickly that a lot of men, once they heard I had a crush on a player, it was over," she says. "They would write me off as just being girly about the whole thing, and think that was the only reason I watched, instead of realizing that it was simply an added bonus."

Britt, a thirty-two-year-old marketing coordinator and San Francisco Giants fan, heartily agrees. "There's absolutely pressure to not be seen as a 'cleat chaser' or just some shallow bimbo—which is bullshit on every conceivable level," she says. "There's so much gatekeeping for female fans in sports, there's a pressure to never do or say anything that could get you kicked out of the club."

Given that men have long dictated the conversation around professional sports, carving out a place for female desire could actually be considered a subversive, even progressive act. But this call for a revolution on frank, open lust raises a fundamental question: Is it sexist to objectify players? Is wanting after them culturally harmful? It shouldn't be, as long as it stays within reasonable, respectful limits. ("I wasn't handing them my underwear," says Mabel. "I just enjoyed from afar.")

Male professional athletes are valued and richly compensated for reasons far beyond their sexual appeal, a luxury not afforded to their female counterparts when it comes to earnings and endorsement deals. Mainstream sports media certainly doesn't exploit male desirability—in fact, it rarely even considers it—nor does it pander to those who desire them. Hotness is a mere accessory, not a necessity, to a male athlete's overall career success; unlike women, they have perceived value beyond some deeply misogynistic, out-of-ten bangability rating on a lad mag website. Their sexual attractiveness isn't systemically oppressing them. (Hell, athletes' wives and girlfriends—generally not public figures like their spouses—are often much more egregiously objectified by the masses.)

What's more interesting is that, when I informally polled a handful of women about their most-desired ballplayers, the diversity of the list was striking. In its totality, it undermined any suggestion that female desire promotes a physical archetype that men are pressured to adhere to. Kevin Kiermaier, Dalton Pompey, Ryan Vogelsong, Troy Tulowitzki, Elvis Andrus, Mitch Moreland, Mark Buehrle, Barry Zito, Cole Hamels, Johnny Damon, Derek Jeter, Prince Fielder, and Brian Dozier all made the list.

Their comments on why these men were their favourites also had a respectful and notably non-dehumanizing sweetness about them: "It looks like his hair would be nice to run your hands through." "He has the prettiest eyes." "His grin is charming and contagious." "His voice is soft, husky and melodious." Many cited how baseball players inspired a sort of innocent desire reminiscent of their early teens, before the complexity and predatory nature of sexism set in. (Think swooning over boy-band members and the thrill of junior-high crushes.) It would seem that the allure was not only for the athlete but also for the safety that the fantasy itself conjured.

"I think the biggest challenge is that we simultaneously want to dispel the myth that all women are into sports because athletes are hot, while also supporting the idea that there's nothing wrong with that," says Britt, the Giants fan. "It's a difficult line to walk."

Maybe a key element of obliterating that line is talking openly and comfortably about how desire fits into this game we so enjoy, a conversation that begins with admitting that it can exist—and that it does. The more sports culture treats women as human beings with feelings and not as some caricature of what women are supposed to be, the more likely the space will become safer and more welcoming for everyone. As absurd as it might seem, the freedom to talk about desire without judgment and dismissal is definitely a part of that.

Out of everyone I spoke to, seventeen-year-old Nationals (and Bryce Harper) fan Nicole offered the most clarity on the issue. "Even though I am painfully shy, baseball has helped me open up and speak in situations I never would have spoken in before," she said. "I have become more confident in my baseball knowledge, so I haven't been as afraid to point out that that guy rakes, and that he's also really hot."

AN ODE TO MARCUS STROMAN

When I have vivid fantasies about the Blue Jays winning the World Series (come on, we all do it), I often think about each individual player's unique reaction. During the 2015 and 2016 seasons, I imagined veteran knuckleball pitcher R.A. Dickey saying something thoughtful, poetic, and subdued, putting his hand to his face and quietly tearing up. I imagined long-overdue-for-a-ring slugger José Bautista with his bat-flipping bravado, cigar firmly in mouth, unafraid to announce to the world that we are indeed the best. I imagined Bringer of Rain Josh Donaldson proud, confident, yet still totally stunned that we came this far.

And then I imagined Marcus Stroman.

If you saw the photos and videos from the Blue Jays' reluctant celebration on September 26, 2015, after securing a playoff berth for the first time in twenty-two years (reluctant because yes, they were going to the playoffs, but they hadn't yet won their division), you'll know exactly what I'm getting at. Stroman, who was only two years old the last time the franchise saw postseason baseball, could easily be described as the happiest human being alive if you go by that beer-soaked footage. He's caught yelling and cheering, full-out dancing to "Trap Queen," taking selfies with teammates, mouth open wide in gleeful celebration. (That guy has the greatest smile, hands down.) It's clear he isn't exactly the type to quip "no big deal" and keep his baseball feelings hidden, and his feelings in that moment are without a doubt unrestrained elation. For me, his enthusiasm—whether he's being sprayed with a can of Bud Lite in the clubhouse, or he's on the mound for an important out—mirrors our own fan hysteria more than any other player on the team. We've seen our own authentic citywide joy in his face, and that joy seems limitless.

Stroman had good reason to celebrate unreservedly—at one point, he wasn't supposed to be on the mound at all. He was our big hope at the beginning of 2015—our potential Opening Day ace—and he spoke fondly in spring training of his relationship with then thirty-five-year-old pitcher Mark "Papa" Buehrle, who was teaching him how to be a pro. During the preseason, Stroman confidently told the media, "I've dealt with a ton of adversity already in my career. Honestly, I feel like there's nothing out there that I can't deal with at this point."

Only a few days after that oddly prescient sound bite, a torn ACL during a practice bunt play appeared to dash all that optimism. "He hit the floor and he held his knee. It was just something you never want to see," said close teammate Aaron Sanchez. "My stomach hurt instantly." When the team announced his injury, and told us he would not come back during the upcoming season, people actually wept. And ever-emotive Stroman tweet-wept right along with us.

"Marcus is the kind of individual you just gravitate around, just because of his attitude and how good of a person he is," veteran catcher Russell Martin told the media at the time. "He has good energy, and when you see a guy like that go down it's tough. Especially a young kid with a whole lot of promise."

It would appear that, with all his good energy, Stroman simply refused to go down. All reports suggest he threw himself completely into rehabilitation, sometimes spending four hours a day in what sportswriter John Lott called an "arduous" program. Immediately after the injury, Stroman decided to use his spare time to complete his sociology degree at Duke University, writing his final research paper on the topic of representations of men and women in sports media. (Stroman eventually picked up his diploma, between starts no less, at the university's May 2016 graduation ceremony.)

And then, during the second game of a soggy September 12 doubleheader, against all possibility and with his family supportively screaming in the stands,

Stroman returned to pitch an important win against the New York Yankees.

"Never give up on your dreams," "Hard work pays off," "Don't lose faith"—Stroman is the unlikely embodiment of every pat inspirational phrase you can think of, and at the risk of hyperbole, he's made a whole city believe in miracles.

The first time I ever saw Stroman pitch was during 2014 spring training. I was down in Florida for my annual baseball pilgrimage, and he was invited for the first time after being ranked the number three prospect in the organization. I will readily admit that the real reason I liked Stroman right away is because of his diminutive size. At 180 pounds and a mere 5'8", he's unusually small for a pitcher, which gives him an immediate likability, an underdog quality, a kind of "disadvantage" that is so easy for many of us to identify with. He even trademarked the acronym *HDMH*, or "Height Doesn't Measure Heart," and speaks fondly of his late grandmother and how she often asserted that good things come in small packages.

"I like beating the odds," he told the *National Post* in 2013. "I'm never going to be one to sit here and say I wish I was six foot. I like being 5'8". That's fine with me."

Stroman didn't exactly give great performances during those initial, meaningless spring games, but he was hard not to love and believe in. Watching him pitch was like watching potential in human form—he was passionate and driven, fun and lighthearted, snapping a wad of pink bubble gum and throwing with surprising control for someone so young. Ever one to bounce back, he eventually proved himself and made his major-league debut as a starter in May 2014, delivering a perfect first inning and a 12–2 win for the Jays over the Kansas City Royals.

Coming as he did from the small town of Stony Brook, New York, and having an unconventional physique when it comes to baseball, people told Stroman he would never make it—yet there he was, pitching a win in the majors. He's famously described himself as the type that doesn't worry. He says he always has a smile on his face, that he's rarely in a bad mood, that he tries to enjoy every moment. He doesn't stress, he doesn't get mad, and he doesn't hold grudges. The one chip he does carry on his shoulder (literally—he got it tattooed) is for those who said he wouldn't make it, that he was too small, that he wouldn't amount to anything.

In June 2016, when facing a slump in his performance, Stroman's good nature didn't waver. After posting a 7.59 ERA over seven starts, there were murmurs in the baseball community about whether he should be sent down to the minors or, worse, that this once reliable wunderkind never really had the stuff to be called an ace after all. While many wanted to write him off as an upstart whose ego didn't match his talent, his positivity persisted, and he was ever confident he could get back on track.

"I see everything anyone says about me," he told ESPN. "I read the blogs. I read the tweets. That's fuel. That's motivation. I see people say I should be sent to [Triple-A] Buffalo, that I should be in the bullpen, that I shouldn't be in the majors . . . They're the ones who said [because] I'm 5-foot-8 . . . I was too short to be a starting pitcher. Now I'm struggling, and I'm hearing it all again. Fine. I like to have those doubters in my life."

On July 6, 2016, only a few days after that interview, Stroman threw a perfect game through five innings against the Royals, and allowed just three hits over eight.

Even when Stroman is not at his best on the mound, he remains a human metaphor for overcoming obstacles. He's a living ray of sunshine—an accessible, personable prodigy who could likely write a book packed with inspirational life advice. For the more pessimistic among us (myself included), his entire public persona is an admirable lesson in how faith and belief in oneself can pull you through the hardest times, a lesson that we're happy to celebrate despite our cynical selves.

In proving the doubters wrong, Stroman has become a sort of stand-in for our own shaky belief in doing things against the odds, against what people tell us isn't possible, whether it's because of a torn ACL or something far less tangible. At only twenty-five years old, the right-handed pitcher with the radiant smile has evolved into the kind of person we want to emulate—he's confident but not cocky, and when the pressure is on he doesn't fold, but instead is compelled to do and be better.

Who wouldn't want that kind of strength for themselves?

"There's going to be people outside of the game who are going to make more ignorant comments. Those don't really affect me. It's the people that matter, the people that are around, the people that are involved in the game. I want to make sure, if it's going to be negative, it's about what I'm saying, not about who I am."

JESSICA MENDOZA

the first female analyst in MLB postseason history

"When hitters are struggling, and you give up on them, then where does that get you? Nowhere."

JOHN GIBBONS

"No matter how many times you say you're sorry, somebody is not going to hear you."

PETE ROSE

"If at first you don't succeed try, try, try, try, try, try, try, try, try, try, try, try again."

JUSTIN VERLANDER

on Twitter

THE POLITICS OF BOOING

On April 25, 2016, Detroit Tigers outfielder Tyler Collins flipped fans the bird.

After he lost a routine fly ball in the lights at home field, fans at Comerica Park responded to Collins's minor mistake with a hearty chorus of boos. Collins retaliated to the derision with the standard obscene gesture and, if you believe the lip reading, a hearty "fuck everybody here, fuck them all." (For what it's worth, the Tigers went on to win against the Oakland A's, 7–3.)

After the game, Collins of course effusively apologized, because that's what professional athletes are supposed to do. "I'm absolutely embarrassed that happened and I'm very sorry to everybody in Detroit," he said. (The idea of *everybody in Detroit* being offended is kind of hilarious, if you ask me.) While Major League Baseball decided not to suspend Collins for his little outburst, he was subsequently demoted to Triple-A, a decision that, given his generally poor performance at the time, probably didn't have a huge amount to do with his middle-finger shenanigans. In fact, the Tigers even came out and said as much.

Because baseball is a game where everyone has an opinion, and those opinions constantly fill our feeds and airwaves, there was a lot of discussion of how it was a big deal that Collins "disrespected fans" with his middle finger. Many said that he should have been stoic, stood there quietly, accepted thousands booing his understandable slip up, and not disgraced the game with his unabashed obscenity. But beyond whether or not the middle finger is naughty, I've thought a lot about how this incident speaks to a culture of fan entitlement and, if I may, the "politics of booing."

I loathe the act of booing. Almost every time it happens during a game, whether I'm in the stadium or watching on television, I find it cringeworthy and grotesque. In extreme cases, it's done for the most nonsensical reasons imaginable—a default, groupthink reaction without any thought toward its own ridiculousness. For example, I couldn't for the life of me understand why, when former Blue Jay Brett Lawrie returned to the Rogers Centre after being traded, he was worthy of a liberal booing during his first at-bat. Is he a traitor because he was exchanged for our American League MVP third baseman, Josh Donaldson? Do we hate him because we're "supposed to"? (To be honest, that would be hard for me, because he's such a ridiculous delight.) Beyond it simply being mean, it seems to me that booing is often the laziest, most robotic fan response, primarily used by ballpark-goers who don't really care about baseball—or basic kindness—and who only care about winning at all costs.

The month after Collins made his gaffe, Blue Jays pitcher Brett Cecil—who was getting a substantial booing of his own, courtesy of fair-weather fans—spoke to the press about his thoughts on the ugly reception. "One thing I will say," Cecil told Postmedia. "If you're going to boo me, don't cheer me when I'm pitching good." Cecil's throwaway comment is actually one weighted with meaning, getting to the heart of what fandom should be all about: *stick with your guys, even when they're struggling.*

On rare occasions, I do find a hearty boo understandable. I get why it happens during egregiously unfair ump calls, or when players are deliberately hit with pitches, or during almost-balks and repeated pickoff attempts. I certainly empathize with booing a player who has committed actual heinous, criminal acts off the field, or when it's a genuine reply to bullshit plays or bad behaviour. We all get excited and emotional sometimes, and we can be forgiven for that. But generally I find the act of booing, especially your own team, the worst kind of fan entitlement.

I have long thought that we collectively demand far too much from baseball players. We demand their time via the media, autograph sessions, and scheduled public appearances. We demand that their sole focus always be on winning, regardless of what is happening in their lives. (Birth of child? Sick relative? Who cares!) For some reason, we think that because we spend our leisure time on baseball, those on the field owe us something more than a game played. We act like players deserve a higher level of abuse—and a lower level of dignity—just because they get paid a lot of money to do something they love.

Not many people think about the fact that it probably doesn't feel very good for a player (who is likely already disappointed in himself) to stand in a stadium and be booed at, just as not many people think of elite athletes as actual human beings. We ask for their best performance every single game, despite the fact that, logically, that's impossible. Booing represents a belief that because we paid some money for a ticket and a beer, we're allowed to scold someone who is slumping. Perhaps even more important, booing suggests they don't deserve our support when they're facing difficulty.

Further, the fact that the status quo argument is that players shouldn't respond but should just "take it," lest they be accused of disrespecting a group of drunk jerks who paid a few bucks for the pleasure of demoralizing another human being, makes me livid. I'm not saying that Collins had a right to say "fuck you" during a nationally televised event (think of the children, blah blah blah), but the fact that the blame was placed solely on his refusal to be a fan punching-bag is a pretty sad commentary on what we think the rights of the average ballpark patron are.

"They have no idea, and that's kind of the part that angers me. A lot of people don't understand the preparation that goes into a lot of pro sports, yet they feel entitled to do stupid stuff like that," Brett Cecil told Postmedia of his own experience with being booed. "Those are the types of things that bother me . . . they don't know the hard work that we as a team and we as individuals put in and yet they still do stupid stuff."

This widespread impulse to turn on one's own team is probably one of the things I hate most about sports. No one is ever allowed to make a mistake, or have a slow couple of weeks, or they'll be rejected by the masses in a chorus of "get rid of him." When I'm at a game and I have to listen to some guy behind me drone on and on about how we should fire John Gibbons, or that Brett Cecil sucks and should be cut, or that R.A. Dickey is garbage and totally done, I'm filled with a kind of raging sadness.

Maybe it's my fault for loving these guys so much, for caring about them through good times and bad, even if I don't know them personally. But despite the fact that these men are just strangers to me, I don't think they—or anyone else, really—deserve to be insulted, mocked, or booed by the masses, no matter how much money they earn. Because there's no mistake that can be made on the field, no performance so bad, no loss so disappointing that it hurts me more than listening to a "fellow fan" gratuitously insult my team's players. Sure, I don't think someone like Collins should flip off thousands of fans, but I don't think he should be sacrificed on an apologetic altar of "respecting the game" either.

MOVING FORWARD WITHOUT FORGETTING: MAJOR LEAGUE BASEBALL AND DOMESTIC VIOLENCE

Many years ago, when I made my first visit to the sexual assault and domestic violence care centre, the intake nurse sat down with me at her desk and searched online for the face of the man who had harmed me.

Her gesture was a meaningful one. I had seen in the news how awful the process of criminal justice can be for survivors, I knew how hard it had been on people in my life who'd tried to pursue it, and I had no intention of going to the police. This was her way of showing me that, regardless of what I decided to do, who I decided to tell, and what played out over the coming months and years, at least one understanding person would know the identity of my abuser and what he had done to me. I remember she told me, with that picture of him on her computer screen, that she knew the names and faces of so many perpetrators of violence.

Businessmen and journalists. Schoolteachers and professional athletes. Friends, husbands, and fathers. "Really nice, likeable guys."

I now go through my life holding on to the memory of that woman, what her acknowledgement of violence meant to me at the time, and what it still means now. I remind myself that while the man who harmed me is happy, has a successful career and a life unimpeded by the violation that upended my own, at least someone, somewhere, will always know what he did.

For those of us who have endured abuse at the hands of someone we loved and trusted, the discussion around José Reyes's June 2016 reunion with the New York Mets—after a suspension for domestic violence and subsequently being dumped by the Colorado Rockies—is one fraught with personal emotion. It is not an abstract baseball debate, nor some logic puzzle to be solved. It's more like opening an old wound that will never completely heal.

On October 31, 2015, José Bernabé Reyes allegedly grabbed Katherine Ramirez, his wife of eight years, by the throat and shoved her into a sliding glass door at the Maui hotel in which they were staying. I'm using the term *allegedly* here because Reyes has never been convicted of the crime, even though, in coded language, he has taken some ownership of the incident, and offered a lacklustre public apology for it at least twice. (Most recently he said, "I feel sorry for what happened. I'm a human being. People make mistakes. For me, I stand up for the terrible mistake that I made.") Further, he served a fifty-one game suspension for violating Major League Baseball's domestic violence policy, and although he had a right to appeal the suspension, he chose not to.

In the 911 call from that evening, a hotel-security staff member told the dispatcher that an argument had occurred, and that Ramirez had suffered injuries to her face, neck, and leg. Reyes was arrested, and Ramirez was aided by medics before being taken to Maui Memorial Medical Center for further treatment. Five months later, prosecutors moved to dismiss the charges against Reyes on the grounds that his wife was refusing to co-operate. He had been scheduled to go to trial less than a week later, on April 4, 2016, Major League Baseball's Opening Day.

Ramirez, of course, deserves no judgment or blame here, and her decision is one that many survivors of violence will deeply understand. While I won't endeavour to assume any of her motivations, I readily acknowledge that her emotional well-being and security, and that of her children, were certainly at stake. For Ramirez, like so many before her, not pursuing criminal justice became the better personal choice. It was one that was hers alone to make—just like forgiveness is hers alone to give.

So what then is the responsibility of baseball fans when it comes to José Reyes? The standard chorus of "innocent until proven guilty" has abated now that he is "standing up" for his "mistake," but the baseball community must still contend with what to do with—or how to appropriately punish, rehabilitate, and, now that he has been unloaded by the Rockies and snapped up by the Mets, cheer for—a player who has harmed someone closest to him, someone he pledged to love and keep safe.

We don't currently have a roadmap for these kinds of conversations. Had Ramirez made the difficult decision to co-operate with investigators, and had Reyes been convicted, it would be different, and perhaps easier to talk about. Culturally we often rely on the courts to tell us what to believe about a person's character, but with a crime like intimate partner violence—one so underreported, and with so many barriers to prosecution—we have to find new ways to discuss appropriate resolution.

Reyes's was one of the first major cases to fall under Major League Baseball's newly implemented domestic violence policy, with its revolutionary clause that a legal conviction is not required for the league to take action. It's a policy that seems to understand that while the justice system doesn't always properly serve victims and rehabilitate offenders, our cultural institutions have a responsibility to do so. Though Reyes never saw a conviction, baseball commissioner Rob Manfred handed down a suspension without pay that spanned the Rockies' first fifty-one games of the 2016 season, and further ordered Reyes to donate $100,000 to the prevention and treatment of domestic violence.

While the current MLB policy is certainly not perfect, and the league is often criticized for dishing out greater punishments for performance-enhancing drugs or gambling than incidents of domestic violence, their handling of Reyes thus far has admittedly been a huge step forward. As Lindsay Gibbs of ThinkProgress rightly points out, despite numerous arrests and accusations in the previous twenty-five years, no player had ever been suspended by the league for domestic violence, and only a handful disciplined by their teams. In March 2016, Yankees closer Aroldis Chapman became the very first to be penalized, receiving thirty games primarily for "his use of a firearm and the impact of that behavior on his partner." (Chapman also did not see legal repercussions for his actions.) It's worth mentioning here that the Mets and the Yankees were able to get these talented players at bargain prices, taking advantage of terrible circumstances under the guise of giving someone a second chance.

In the case of both Reyes and Chapman, it has been difficult to discern what exactly is "fair," given this is uncharted territory for sports at large. Sadly, real justice is not quantifiable in days, years, or dollars fined. But now that Reyes has served his punishment, the talk is less about implementing policy and more about what kind of reception a player deserves post-suspension, and the flawed narrative of a "triumph over adversity" that is being written about Reyes's return to the Mets—a place where he was much beloved.

As a fan of the Toronto Blue Jays, I can understand the challenge of reconciling the likeable, jovial face of Reyes, and the talent he displays on-field, with the reality of what he has done. I cheered exuberantly for him during the two and a half years he was on "my team," cried when he was injured in 2013, and was disappointed when he was traded to the Colorado Rockies in 2015. Yet none of those prior warm feelings negate the alleged act of violence he committed. Those seeming opposites can exist in the same person—and very often, they do. Abusers can be "nice, likeable guys." Those of us who have been abused, or have witnessed abuse, understand all too well that nice guys hurt women all the time. Abusers are not convenient monster-caricatures that are easy to spot and steer clear of. More often they are our friends. They are kind and smiling, well-liked and lauded, because that's exactly the kind of person you allow to get close enough to hurt you.

A key component of Major League Baseball's domestic violence policy—the necessity of counselling—remains somewhat shrouded in mystery, though Reyes has shared with the media that the process has aided him in becoming a better husband, father, and man, and that he's willing to talk to other players about making sure other incidents like this don't happen. "I am encouraged by Mr. Reyes's commitment to the treatment provisions of the Policy in order to ensure that such an incident does not occur in the future," Manfred said upon handing down the suspension.

Yes, Reyes should absolutely be given the tools to become "a better person" via the institutions that have accepted him back into the fold. If they seek to benefit from his athletic skill, they have to accept valid criticism and take responsibility for what he has done—for what he has the capacity to do. Fans should also continuously hold these institutions, and the outlets that cover them, accountable, because if not us, who will? Language is important, and Reyes's actions shouldn't be rewritten—as is so common in sports media—as simply adversity to overcome. His act of violence shouldn't be referred to, as a *New York Times* headline clumsily called it, as "baggage." What has happened should not be blotted from memory by his performance on the field, and despite what the scrum sound bites tell us, *he didn't make a "mistake"—he made a choice*. This isn't a "public relations problem," this is about the vital recognition of an act of violence, one that doesn't go away simply because we want to cheer for a team we love. Our team loyalties, and our desire to be comfortable watching the game, don't supersede the violation of another human being.

My gut says that if it were up to me, Reyes would no longer be allowed to play major-league baseball. He would never again be allowed to enjoy the game he loves, to be cheered on by fans and teammates, or to enjoy the fame, money, and glory that goes along with that. He would not be allowed to tarnish what, for me and so many other survivors, has become a source of solace and escape. But I also understand that's not my decision to make, and instead of lamenting the easily detestable choices of the Mets organization and blindly cheering fans, I am trying to see a positive way forward.

We can't be inside Reyes and Ramirez's relationship. We can't know if he is genuinely sorry, or if he really will endeavour to change. We can simultaneously understand that we want him to disappear completely from baseball, and recognize, as it stands now, that is simply not possible—just like it's not always possible for our own abusers to disappear completely from *our* lives. Instead we have to focus on ongoing restorative and preventative action, one that serves survivors and rehabilitates offenders.

As hard as it is to acknowledge, if Reyes was not in professional baseball he would simply be somewhere else—likely somewhere where he would be held less accountable for his actions, where he would lack the necessary resources and systems to ensure that his abusive behaviour doesn't happen again. Rehabilitation and prevention are important things to keep in mind when faced with the knowledge that close to five million women in the U.S. will experience physical violence by an intimate partner every year, and one in four will become a victim of severe violence by an intimate partner in their lifetime.

For every fan who knows all too well how difficult the aftermath of abuse can be, it can be painful and upsetting to hear fans enthusiastically chant Reyes's name and beg for his autograph. There's a mix of rage and sadness in watching the media and the MLB powers that be blot out his actions with euphemisms, stats, and manufactured narratives. It's heavy with the understanding that it takes both time and open dialogue to discern what is the best, restorative course of action—and reaction—for victims and abusers, for fans and teams. As much as we would like it to be otherwise, the story of violence against women doesn't end at punishment; instead it continues in the daily experience of what cannot be undone.

The painful reality is that there is no satisfying, tidy resolution to be had here—but there are ways forward via ongoing, open dialogue. There is also our very human responsibility to create a space where education, change, and the prevention of violence are finally possible in sports. And despite how much fans might want to turn away, have a good time, and win some games, there is a real onus on all of us to keep talking, and never forget what has been done.

DISPATCHES FROM SPRING TRAINING

March 10, 2016

There's something about looking forward to your first spring training game of the year that reminds me of an eagerly awaited romantic date with a loved one. There's a hell of a lot of buildup and anticipation during those preceding, terrible months without baseball, a lot of wondering about what the day will look and feel like, a lot of nervous yet optimistic energy buzzing around as you eagerly take to the Florida interstate that will finally reunite you with your beloved. In fact, I'd be lying if I told you I didn't always carefully pick out my outfit the night before game day.

For diehard fans, getting back to the ballpark—any ballpark—after a wintery five-month hiatus can be pretty emotional. If that reunion happens in Florida, there's a good chance that the weather will be beautiful and the mood congenial, making it hard not to get teary behind your sunglasses as you push through the turnstile for the very first time that year. All of that emotion is only heightened when the last time you saw your dream date he was gunning hard for a spot in the World Series.

Spring training games may be, as they so often say, meaningless, but after the triumph, the anxiety, the elation, and the heartbreak that fans of the Toronto Blue Jays endured during the playoffs in October 2015, it's hard not to carry all our lofty expectations with us into every matchup in the spring.

My 2016 reunion with the Toronto Blue Jays didn't happen at the team's springtime home in Dunedin, but instead at Tampa's George M. Steinbrenner Field, one of the Grapefruit League's more majestic and polished ballpark offerings. Steinbrenner is a tinier model of Yankee Stadium, still steeped in all its heritage and holiness though the capacity is about one-fifth its parent's size. (It is, however, the largest spring training ballpark in Florida.) From the sprawling $10 open-field parking lot, which is staffed primarily by polite retirees, the park is a quick walk across the bridge over Route 92. The stadium itself is tastefully decorated with a collection of pennants, each marking a year in which the storied Yankees won a World Series—there are twenty-seven in all, if you're masochistic and counting.

In my regular life, I'm annoyingly early to pretty much everything—meetings, appointments, parties, you name it. (It's a pain for everyone involved.) Baseball games are of course no exception; I absolutely have to be in my seat in time for the national anthems, and I also like to get there early enough for a good stroll of the concourse, especially in an unfamiliar stadium. Game time today in Tampa is 1:05 p.m., but I'm already through the gate by 11:00 a.m. and eager to take in every last drop of the ballpark experience before the first pitch is thrown. As I tour Steinbrenner, making my way down the aisles toward the field, dozens of yellow-shirted staffers, most of whom are seniors, say hello and tell me that they hope I enjoy the game. It's such a pleasant environment that for a pessimist like me the scene feels almost suspect, as if it's impossible for all of these people to be this nice in quick succession without any nefarious motives.

As the stadium fills up, I watch as a guy in a Jays jersey has a warm, friendly chat with a guy in a Yankees jersey, a good visual reminder that during spring training there are no immediate pressing rivalries (they'll be dealt with later), the clock is back to zero, and the slate is wiped clean. We're all just loving baseball for what it is, all over again.

The real bonus of arriving early to spring training games is the proximity it gives you to the players: there are already a handful of fans congregating along the third-base line to get a closer look at Troy Tulowitzki, Russell Martin, Josh Donaldson, and Kevin Pillar. Those boys in blue casually exercise as frantic onlookers snap photos, and lucky children occasionally get a ball tossed their way. While the fans collectively lurk, an elderly Steinbrenner staffer warns the enthusiastic adults that they need to make sure only children occupy the first row, lest everyone be told to take a hike.

In a nice confluence of events, my first game of the year also marks José Bautista's return to the field for the first time since the Kansas City Royals eliminated the Jays in Game Six of the 2015 American League Championship Series. Watching the future free agent do his pregame yoga-style stretches is a meditative experience, and I can't help but join in the hearty chorus of "pay the man whatever he wants" while witnessing him methodically prep for this particular spring game. After Bautista finishes his toe touches and back stretches, he wanders toward batting practice and joins Josh Donaldson as they crack balls far into the outfield. Heartthrob Donaldson has somehow managed to modify his uniform ever so slightly, solidifying his bad boy status by pulling his baseball pants up to his knees (sans high socks) and positioning his cap off-kilter and high on his head. He's apparently in charge of the pregame music, with a tiny portable speaker in his hip pocket blaring out team-pleasing tunes with a little something for everyone.

For the following nine innings, I'm stationed out in left field, my seatmates a couple of kindly Yankees fans from Tulsa, Oklahoma. We strike up a convivial conversation immediately, and I'm fascinated by the fact that they've managed to become fans of the pinstripes despite hailing from a city more than 2,000 kilometres from N.Y.C. They tell me they're both close to sixty years into their Yankees fandom, and that they got impromptu-married in Las Vegas the year the Twins beat the Cardinals in the World Series (1987). She laughs when she points out theirs is actually her seventh marriage, the one that finally stuck, after all the others lasted less than a year a piece. As the game progresses, they teach me about the Yankees players I know little about, and I do the same for them about the Jays.

In the grand scheme of baseball things, there was nothing exceptional about this particular Thursday game at Steinbrenner. People were nice and the weather was a perfect 24 degrees and sunny. I drank a summer shandy out of a plastic Yankees souvenir cup, ate some $6 popcorn, and sang the holy song of "Take Me Out to the Ball Game" for the first time in far too long. Drew Hutchison, looking to secure a fifth starter spot during the regular season, allowed two runs and three hits over two and a bit innings. Aroldis Chapman, facing a thirty-day regular-season suspension under MLB's new domestic violence policy, hit Bautista with a pitch in the fifth. Twenty-sixth-ranked prospect Andy Burns blasted a three-run homer over the wall in left field. Josh Donaldson was—as always—talented, endlessly entertaining, MVP-calibre Josh Donaldson.

When it was all done Bautista told the media, "It was fine; normal first game." But the game was altogether beautiful, as baseball games always are. If I were the kind of person who believes in cosmic messages (I am), an 11–4 win over the Yankees at my first game of 2016 bodes pretty well for the postseason future. It's worth noting that the Jays currently have the best record in the Grapefruit League, with eight wins, one loss, and a tie.

Even though I know it's all supposedly meaningless, it sure as hell felt like a damn good first date.

March 11, 2016

Before rookie Jays outfielder Dalton Pompey took his first at-bat at today's game against the Boston Red Sox, he chatted through the netting with the guy in the seat next to me about how they both went to the same Mississauga high school. That, my friends, is how small Florida Auto Exchange Stadium in Dunedin actually is.

The game was the first sellout of the spring season for the Blue Jays' southern home base, meaning just over 5,000 people bought a seat to check out Marcus Stroman's

Friday start. (For some idea of scale, that's one-tenth the size of the Rogers Centre.)

Florida Auto Exchange Stadium may not be the most glamorous of the Grapefruit League's offerings, but it certainly has its rundown, back-to-basics charms. Built in 1990, the stadium holds a mere 5,509 people, offering them a bustling, tented, outdoor barbecue, a handful of tiny beer stations, and lots of complimentary sunscreen.

"Delightful Dunedin" itself is the very definition of a sleepy small town, and is officially one of the tiniest that Major League Baseball uses for training purposes. Down in Dunedin's famous, cigarette smoke–filled and draft beer–scented dive bar Bauser's, which is a short stroll from the park, you can get "free beer with parking"—a sketchy promise on a handwritten sign that has come to define the whole vibe for me. If the beer doesn't entice you, you can take advantage of parking deals offered by locals, each trying to make a quick buck by getting you to park in their driveway. The culture of Dunedin really seems to be governed by the Jays, with the team's logo appearing everywhere—on welcome signs, street banners, and on the T-shirt of the nice lady who serves you your breakfast.

The stadium's diminutive scale means the distance between you and the field of play shrinks considerably. Today I splurged on front-row seats behind home plate—a whole $25—which meant I was close enough to see that

Russell Martin's ankle guard is emblazoned with his last name. Seeing your favourite players from this vantage point has the benefit of revealing their humanity in a way a huge stadium never could. It reminds you that they're really just men, though highly talented, incredibly skilled, really athletic men. In fact, when one heckler behind me loudly suggested twenty-five-year-old utility infielder Andy Burns wouldn't make the team, I almost turned around and told him to keep it down, just in case Burns overheard.

At every Dunedin game, a lucky child is plucked from the stands to yell a "play ball!" Today he stood awkwardly yet enthusiastically next to the Jays' mascot, Ace, proudly wearing his tiny jersey and yelling the hallowed, ceremonial words into a microphone before the players we missed all winter took to the field.

Watching Marcus Stroman run out to the mound from where I was sitting was a rare thing of beauty—and honestly I feel like it's a gift to even be able to witness his work at all. From that short distance you come to better understand the sheer power of his pitches, his unshakable focus, and the complexity of the subtle gestures that are passed back and forth between him and his catcher. Generally, starters only do a handful of innings at a time during spring training, but on this particular Friday, Stroman stuck around longer than expected. There was a moment when you could see he knew that he would be pulled shortly, and he started to give everything he had to close out his "meaningless" performance. When he eventually made his exit, he got a standing ovation from fans above the dugout.

Spring training games are often a perfect place to indulge in one's passion for the art of pitching. You get to spend a little time with a familiar face like veteran Brett Cecil's, see a youngster like twenty-one-year-old Roberto Osuna do a long Catholic prayer and sign of the cross on the mound, or check out a new acquisition like Drew Storen, a reliever rescued from the Washington Nationals. This day's particular highlight was seeing "submariner" Ben Rowen toss from the mound—the unconventional right-hander throws with an incredibly distinctive style that is a quirky joy to behold. In fact, today really drove home how wonderfully diverse a team's pitching staff can be, like a glorious island of misfit baseball toys: there's the resurrected 5'8" wunderkind whose height doesn't measure heart in Stroman, the ambidextrous anomaly with the six-finger glove in Pat Venditte, the survivor knuckleballer with the missing ligament in R.A. Dickey, and now the player with the weird and wonderful upside-down release in Rowen.

That former Mississauga high schooler beside me spent the day teaching his six-year-old son about the game, fielding his endless, endearing questions with incredible patience. "What team did Drew Storen play on before?"

"Which player has been an All-Star the most times?" "Will Marcus Stroman be an All-Star this year?" "What does stealing signs mean?" I ultimately laughed with said dad when I realized he had started making his answers up, too tired to tell his curious kid he no longer had any idea what he was talking about. More than any other baseball environment, spring training is a place where your seatmates easily become your friends. Everyone has made a personal pilgrimage and has a great story to tell about how their love of the game inspired them to journey so many miles. They are devotees eager to share their passion and excitement with fellow travellers, a congregation of "your people" whose vibrant chatter finally breaks the long silence of a baseball-less winter.

The Red Sox tied it up 1–1 at the top of the ninth inning, and the umpires made the call to go into extras. (A tie is not an uncommon call during spring training, with everyone opting to go home instead of slugging it out indefinitely.) Even the most devoted of baseball fans will have a hard time recognizing the name of every player who appears in the lineup toward the end of the game—the superstars tend to have gone to the showers, while lesser-known hopefuls play on until the last out. You would think this might be a disappointment, but instead it's a fun and wonderful reminder of how truly magical this game really is. On Bautista's and Donaldson's days off, or when Martin is already in his car, I find myself more than happy to stay on and watch a walk-off care of a stranger.

The last time I saw a Blue Jays walk-off game in person was when Josh Donaldson blasted a homer out of the Rogers Centre during the last home game of the 2015 regular season. This tenth-inning walk-off—an RBI single from minor-leaguer Jon Berti—was decidedly less dramatic but, at its core, no less satisfying. In the end, it's the game we really love—whether it's played out in a packed, delirious, electric Rogers Centre during the playoffs, or here in this tiny town that gives you a free beer just for parking your car in one of their lots.

After a high-stakes season, and the abyss that follows it, Dunedin has a nice way of getting you right back to baseball basics.

"It was my first lesson as a pro ballplayer that I needed to stay true to myself and who I am to have success. Even today my manager, Brad Ausmus, always tells me, 'Don't try to be Clayton Kershaw or Justin Verlander. Be Daniel Norris, because that's the reason you're here.'"

DANIEL NORRIS

"I think it's only human that you question some of the methods and you question some of the selections. Or you go back and watch tape and you think I should have done this differently or whatnot. But at the end of the day, if I've learned anything through my experiences as a baseball player, it's that you kind of got to have blinders on and trust the pedigree. I know it's in there."

R.A. DICKEY

on giving up home runs in 2016

"I believe you've got to utilize what God gave you, so if you have facial hair, there are ways to look good while sporting it."

JOSÉ BAUTISTA

(of course)

ADAM LIND IS TRADED, LONG LIVE ADAM LIND

In November 2014, the Toronto Blue Jays traded my favourite player. During the hot, beer-clutching days at the ballpark the summer prior, I mostly chose to disregard the sad rumblings of that fated certainty. It's easy to ignore all the conjecture when the AstroTurf is green and you've got a two-can buzz on, but the idea of the coming loss still lingers deep in the back of your mind. You imagine what he would look like in another team's uniform, vaguely try to picture visiting his new team's ballpark, and anticipate the pangs of jealousy you will feel hearing another fanbase yelling his name, but like any anxious thought it's safer not to entertain it until it's true and final.

On November 1, Adam Lind's option was exercised, and that same day he became a Milwaukee Brewer. Lind, who up until that day was the longest-serving current member of the Blue Jays baseball club, was my "favourite player" for about four seasons. I like to think that's a relationship weighty enough to justify the absurd little breakup-style cry I had when news of the trade hit. I salved the burn of loss with thoughts about him hanging out with Hank—the famed Brewers dog and unofficial mascot—daydreamed about a Cactus League spring training trip, and wondered what I would do with my now-defunct Adam Lind jersey. I also reflected heavily on this strange relationship we have with the ballplayers who top our personal lists, these total strangers we come to love—and who we are suddenly expected to turn our backs on out of loyalty to our geographical home base. In my shock that shouldn't have been a shock at all, I thought about the embarrassing despondency we feel upon their departure, the inexplicable pain that forces us to examine the very nature of fandom.

I will readily admit that Lind was not my favourite during his days as an anointed Silver Slugger, and that I missed the crazed fanfare of the early years when his bat burned the hottest. The year 2011 marked my return to baseball after a lengthy break, so I wasn't there on that record-setting day in 2009, when Lind was the Opening Day designated hitter and drove in six runs against the Detroit Tigers, giving Roy Halladay the win. I was absent during the era when Lind was so easy to love; instead I found him compelling at a time when the general populace had mostly given up on him, when all his stats had slumped into a set of numbers that made him at best reliable, mostly average, and occasionally the victim of an unforgiving, ugly chorus of "you suck."

I chose Lind in 2011 for the inexplicable, amorphous, and very personal reasons we each pick out our favourite players—reasons that seem to differ dramatically from fan to fan. That year was, to put it mildly, terrible for me, and it was that terribleness that prompted my return to baseball. I found comfort again in the innocuous yet beautiful dramas of the game, near-randomly plucking Lind out of the roster as the player I would label my own. The strange chemistry of that connection always seems to be an indiscernible alignment of both where that player is and where we are in our own lives. Some of us lazily choose "the best," while others need to see promise in unlikely heroes. Some of us gravitate toward underdogs, while others like more obvious fanfare. Some enjoy quirky personalities and general on-field hilarity, while others buy jerseys emblazoned with the names of their team's strong yet silent types. It wouldn't be too far-fetched to say your answer to the question "who's your favourite player?" says a great deal about not only who you are but where you're at in life.

What picking humble, soft-spoken Lind says about me I can't entirely be sure. Perhaps it was because the sports reporters I know never had a bad word to say about him, often telling me he was "smarter than people think," polite, and always up for their questions, even if it seemed he thought some of the questions were absurd (they were, but he'd answer them anyway). In my first and only media scrum with him, he seemed incredibly *human*—adorably self-effacing and genuine, a refreshing sort of superstar who had no idea he was one.

A Midwestern "oh, shucks" stereotype, Lind was the quintessential, likeable nice guy, married to a local girl (from Scarborough, like myself) who took pity on him one night when she saw him eating alone in a Toronto restaurant, all afraid of the big city. "It was a whole new world, man. Nothing like I'd ever experienced before," Lind said of his new home. "Unlike Indiana or Alabama or any of the stops I'd had in the minor leagues."

The slugger was the subject of a collection of similarly endearing stories, like when his mom urged him to get an MRI on a broken foot that the Blue Jays medical staff had missed. He consistently skirted the limelight, and never said or did anything all that outspoken, offensive, or controversial. If he did ever say anything combative, we were only shocked because it came from his mouth. In the end, the sole thing fans argued about when it came to Lind was whether he should keep his long, unkempt, red goatee.

Despite his affable nature, loving Lind was an exercise in masochistic endurance. People were prone to cruelty, calling him lazy and stupid, screaming for a trade on bad days and saying close to nothing on the good ones. He had a definite "phoenix rising from the ashes" quality about him, even if that phoenix seemed to be burning up and rising and burning up and rising over and over again. I vividly recall my tantrum when, on May 17, 2012, the Blue Jays optioned Lind to a Jays Triple-A affiliate in Vegas, and then—unbeknownst to him at the time—followed up by putting him on outright waivers. When he miraculously returned to Toronto a month later, he slowly bounced back, and by June of the following year he had a magical .350 batting average and had temporarily crept onto the list of the top-five American League batting leaders. (I was pretty damn smug during that period of time.)

Support for Lind waxed and waned so much that being consistently committed to him made you feel like a member of an elite cult of believers, regardless of how crazy people thought you were. The payoff was the distinct thrill of being able to say "I told you so," allowing you to relish in his ascension when everyone else had fickly written him off.

In the big blue sea of a Rogers Centre full of Jays fans, the percentage of Lind jerseys was certainly on the lower end during the time I claimed him as "my player." Lawries and Bautistas were abundant, and when I walked the concourse and saw another Lind like my own there was a silly, juvenile impulse to feel a connection with another convert. Liking him also provided me with ritual and structure—I always bought my ball tickets on the first-base line, whether it was at the Rogers Centre, or spring training, or Fenway, or Wrigley, or Comerica. I took great pleasure in the fact that when Lind went yard, people in my life would kindly lie and let me know "he did that for you."

From Lind, I ultimately learned your favourite is like your baseball anchor, a way of returning to each game with glorious predictability, as he stands there on his base, kicking at the bright red dirt.

I often think of my relationship with my favourite ballplayers as similar to the relationship I have with great artists, writers, or filmmakers. What they have produced, over the length of their careers, has had an incredibly positive, buoying, and consoling effect on my life. Their work on the field has saved me during the times I needed saving, has helped me better understand my world and the pain I've endured, and has simply made me happy when I needed a little more happy in my life. And even if I don't know them personally, I can admire, respect, and be grateful to them for the solace they've offered me, win or lose. And I can appreciate how much they have given me, and how generous they have been with those gifts throughout their lives.

Why we love what we love is such predictable fodder for so many lyrical musings on the game of baseball. I've seen enough old men cry over the loss of players, teams, and games over the years to understand that while that strange brand of devotion doesn't have any logical explanation, it is as real as it comes. And when you sign up for being a fan, nobody sits you down and teaches you how to say goodbye to a player, and you'd feel ridiculous for even asking for that lesson. It is, after all, just a game—a strange stew of affection and business that means inevitable heartbreak for us all.

In my grief over losing Lind, it would have been easy for me to hurl invective at then-GM Alex Anthopoulos because he traded my anchor for a song yet to be sung. (For what it's worth, that song turned out to be Marco Estrada, a pitcher who played no small part in the team's subsequent postseason victories.) At the time, it would have been easy to lament the game and the decisions that often seemed to belie my loyalties. But as I moved through the process of mourning, I preferred to be grateful for that dirt-kicking, redheaded Midwestern boy who—during a terrible year—brought me back to baseball. And as he, like so many players before him, bounce around the major leagues, it's where I'll stay, regardless of where he plays.

THE UNHAPPY LESSON OF THE 1993 WORLD SERIES

When I was fourteen years old, Joe Carter hit a now-mythological walk-off home run against the Philadelphia Phillies at the end of the sixth (and final) game of the 1993 World Series. The three-run homer was, at the time, certainly the greatest moment in the history of the Blue Jays franchise, and arguably one of the most beautiful and memorable moments in the history of baseball.

I was lucky enough to be in one of Toronto's suburbs that day, after Carter hit it out of the park and was asked by broadcaster Tom Cheek to "touch 'em all, Joe." Jubilant fans poured out of the stadium, and I got in a car with a friend and her older sister so the three of us could join the happy hordes downtown.

Sadly, the only solid memory I really have of October 23, 1993, is that of a grown man making an obscene sexual gesture in my direction during the public celebration that followed the game. With his shaved head and goatee, his tongue darting in and out of his mouth while he loomed above me, that grotesque man is someone I've never forgotten. It was the first time I realized a baseball game was a heaven that sometimes demons broke their way into, and that sports culture was sexist and sometimes even scary.

He taught me that the world of baseball—regardless of how much I would come to love it—could sometimes be an ugly place for people like me.

Even though the details of Carter's legendary home run are etched lovingly in my baseball brain, I've fact-checked the finer details of the above paragraphs more than a dozen times. This is because, as a woman who writes and talks about baseball, I know there's always a man at the ready to tell you that you got it wrong. There's always someone at the ballpark eager to test your knowledge, your fandom, your passion, and your right to be there. There's always someone in the stands who assumes your male partner is the one who really cares about the game, and you're just tagging along for the ride.

And there's always someone to remind you—with their words and their actions—that you simply aren't welcome.

Despite that man's lewd (and frankly terrifying) gesture, in the years since Joe Carter's historic blast I have come to feel that there is nowhere I would rather be than swept up in the electric atmosphere of a live game. Even when baseball is at its most postseason-stressful—with all the anxiety of, say, a 2016 Blue Jays do-or-die wild card game against the well-matched Baltimore Orioles, or the uncertainty that leads up to an ALDS sweep against the Texas Rangers on a Game Three error in extra innings—I revel in how the ballpark can still be a vital source of comfort. For many, baseball provides an escape from the more terrible aspects of our day-to-day lives, acting as a kind of secular church where we come together and faithfully connect over the triumphs and struggles of our team.

And yet, there are those who forget the fundamentally congenial and communal nature of baseball fandom; those who think it's solely about their experience, and who disregard their fellow fans and the generous spirit of the game. During that aforementioned glorious wild card matchup, there were guys to my left in the 200 level at the Rogers Centre who spent much of the evening spouting obscenities and homophobic slurs, and making "fat chick" jokes. And there were the guys to my right who were happy to yell racist garbage at an opposing player, and who repeatedly touched our section's usher without her consent.

And then, of course, there was that one guy who thought it was a good idea to disrupt a crucial seventh-inning play during one of the most important games of the 2016 season by tossing a beer can at Orioles outfielder Hyun-Soo Kim.

Even with all the joy and elation of thrilling victories, with all the strangers I've high-fived and hugged over the years, there have certainly been times when I've felt unsafe at the stadium. In fact, I've encountered groups of dangerous, drunken, and disrespectful men in almost every ballpark I've been to, from San Francisco to Chicago. In the great sea of enthusiastic, kindly fans, it takes only a few thoughtless jerks to create real discomfort.

Everyone deserves to feel safe in a public space, and it takes so little to ensure that sense of well-being: keep your mouth shut when you feel the urge to yell something questionable, keep your hands to yourself, and keep your beer can firmly in your hand. As someone who goes to watch live baseball on a regular basis, I'm no longer surprised by the disrespect sometimes shown to the atmosphere of the ballpark, to the players who populate its field or the fans who cheer them on, but it always pains me to see it. Loving this game, no matter which team you cheer for, sadly means often having to endure offensive fan behaviour, whether it's sexist, racist, or homophobic outbursts; aggressive or even violent conduct; or just a general feeling of unease at the stadium.

And the higher the baseball stakes and ballpark attendance, the more we see this kind of drunken, hateful indifference to basic human decency.

I can't help but think that the biggest problem, when it comes to a toxic ballpark and baseball culture at large, is the apathy of those fans who are not themselves targeted for abuse. I understand that when you hear someone yelling out obscene or hateful things, or you see someone behaving inappropriately, your instinct might be to "mind your own business" and do nothing, if only to avoid causing more trouble or creating any further discomfort. I also know there is a genuine fear that if you intervene, things will escalate, because it's a fear I have certainly felt myself. But the hard fact is we have to stand up for each other and what is right. We have to be part of the solution no matter how uncomfortable it makes us. We have to take a long look at what we can personally do to make the sports community at large more inclusive for all of its members, on both a macro and micro level, especially those who are most vulnerable to abuse and attack.

Maybe that starts by asking some fundamental questions about who is allowed to have a voice in conversations about the game.

A few years ago I subscribed to *Sportsnet Magazine*, and as luck would have it my very first issue was devoted entirely to Major League Baseball. About a quarter of the way through the magazine there was an ad featuring a group shot of what the copy claimed was "Canada's Deepest Roster of Baseball Experts": thirteen (mostly white) men, holding baseball bats and balls, smiling happily into the camera. It struck me that likely not a single man pictured thought "maybe this is a problem" or "maybe this is sending the wrong message." Not one person who shot, designed, or approved that campaign thought to question what the striking image said about the exclusionary state of baseball culture: *This is a game played by men, for men, and talked about by (mostly white) men*. Though I'm sure Sportsnet and its ilk are more than happy to take my money, the optics of that ad suggested they didn't seem interested in carving out a space for female fans like me, or for diverse perspectives in general.

I raise this anecdote not to condemn Sportsnet (it's worth noting they've since added sportscaster Hazel Mae to their roster of baseball experts) but instead to emphasize how much representation matters. It sets the tone for baseball and ballpark culture, and directly affects how those who are excluded feel and are sometimes treated when they take their rightful seats in the stadium. I know all too well that men make up an overwhelming majority of the "respected" voices around sports, and that sometimes simply pointing this fact out can lead to you being maligned, excluded, ridiculed, and, in the worst cases, bullied and abused.

As a woman who loves a sport and yet refuses to accept the status quo, I've had my ideas picked apart, my opinions dismissed, my experiences discounted—all for what is literally "just a game." I'll admit there have been times when I've grown weary of that fight, and tired of fielding the stream of insults or struggling against the frustrating silence of apathy. My anger about the lack of diverse representation in sports media, with all those white male faces on panels and mastheads, and how that skewed perspective on what a baseball expert should look like feeds the undercurrent of misogyny in so many conversations—all of it has led to a dull, debilitating sadness that has tainted this game I so desperately adore. It has made me think a great deal about that fourteen-year-old girl who craved baseball, only to be met with the demoralizing, predatory sexism of a fellow fan.

I really want things to be better—not only for women but for anyone who has felt sports culture's exclusionary sting—but sometimes it feels like the constant yelling from the outside has done little more than wear me out. When I make critiques of sports culture in general, I often have possible solutions at the ready: the media should make diversity its mission, and the sports world as a whole, especially its high-profile white male personalities, should be encouraged to support, mentor, and provide opportunities to women, people of colour, and those who have been consistently shut out. Fans should condemn sexism, racism, and homophobia where and when they see it, and stand up for anyone they see being pushed out, abused, or attacked. But as I continue to hear the same cyclical arguments and the endless excuses for an obvious lack of diversity, my patience has worn thin.

The reality is this: Those who refuse to actively foster a welcoming environment at the ballpark and within sports culture are on the wrong side of history. They are failing. They are doing a bad job. They can say it's hard, or time-consuming, or above and beyond what they're willing to do, but that doesn't negate a responsibility to rise to the challenge.

And it doesn't change the fact that it's egregious to refuse to do anything at all.

More than twenty years after Joe Carter won the World Series with that incredible home run, my beloved Jays finally went back to the postseason. By 2015 I was so far from the teenage girl who revelled in that initial taste of baseball magic, but I still watched those playoff games with the giddiness and unrestrained emotion of youth. I was teary-eyed and riveted as my team won the American League East and battled their way through the ALDS against the Texas Rangers, and was crushed when the Kansas City Royals ultimately eliminated them in the league championship series.

During one of those triumphant playoff games, I exited the glorious buzz of the stadium and joined the celebrating crowd, only to be shoved into a busy street by a drunken, aggressive man with no regard for the people around him. When I protested, he turned to me, looming menacingly above, called me a "bitch," and then went on to make vulgar, inappropriate comments about my body.

I was right back in that place I was decades ago—demoralized, terrified, the joy of baseball momentarily sullied by the actions of someone so thoughtless and cruel. Instead of feeling the elation of victory that I—like anyone else—was entitled to, I was instead entirely deflated. I had long put up a fight to secure my rightful place in the culture of sports, and some drunken idiot had taken it upon himself to remind me that I would never really feel safe. That I would never really belong.

Yet despite how discouraging and upsetting that moment was, I know I have to keep going back to the ballpark, and I have to keep asserting my right and the right of others to be a part of the baseball community. And no matter how hard and tiresome it can be to discuss issues of inclusion, I understand how important it is to do so. This is a fight we all have a responsibility to engage in, if only so a fourteen-year-old girl can safely enjoy a game.

CHEATING, EMPATHY, AND MAKING SENSE OF A PED SUSPENSION

When the news broke in April 2016 that Blue Jays first baseman Chris Colabello had been suspended for eighty games after testing positive for a performance-enhancing substance, someone on Twitter gently asked me if I condoned cheating.

Though the question was jarring, I can certainly understand why it came my way. On social media, I had just extolled the virtues of empathy and understanding when it came to PEDs. I had stated that, yes, it was okay to be sad or disappointed with this news, but I also offered a reminder to vitriolic Jays (and non-Jays) fans that baseball players are human beings and that they make mistakes just like the rest of us.

"Of course I don't condone cheating," was my response.

Unless you are a sociopath, you know that cheating is wrong. It's a fundamental life lesson learned the first time your dad catches you popping a ball into the hole at mini golf when you thought no one was looking. (Guilty, age six.) It's a rule repeated from the playground to the playing field, from elementary school to university. We're told not to butt in front of someone in a lineup, not to take a head start, and not to cut any corners. We're discouraged from looking at a classmate's test, from lifting passages from an essay, or from passing someone else's ideas off as our own. In fact, "never cheat" is generally one of the very first personal codes we're asked to adopt. Cheaters are bad, we're told. They're greedy, selfish people who take shortcuts, want to have it all without earning it, and steal the glory from those who have done the real work. It's usually a pretty black-and-white tenet of human interaction, one intended to uphold an even playing field and ensure that only those who deserve it achieve success, fame, and acclaim.

Yet, like it or not, the realm of cheating can involve many shades of grey, if only because the world is not as equitable, or as fair, as we would like to believe. This doesn't mean that cheating within the world of sports should be condoned or given a pass, or that we should try to make excuses for it. It simply means that it's okay to look at each case in context, and attempt to understand why cheating might become something that an athlete feels they need to do. Do people cheat because they live in fear of losing their hard-won status? Because their livelihood and their identity are at stake? What kind of burden must exist, especially in the world of professional sports, to make cheating a risky yet viable option?

Given how frequently PED infractions happen in Major League Baseball (nine during the 2016 season, and thirty-five since 2010), making an effort to understand the impulse—or at least be open-minded when it comes to having a conversation about it—might be our best bet for figuring out how to prevent them.

The hard and fast rule of "cheaters are bad people" would be easy to uphold if there weren't myriad forces at work that drive otherwise ethical people to make questionable choices; if we genuinely lived in a meritocracy; if privilege didn't give some individuals an inherent head start over others in life. Some people cheat not out of maliciousness or selfishness, but out of fear, desperation, and a need to retain their precarious accomplishments, livelihoods, or reputations. The reality is that each offender brings his own complex motivation to using nefarious means to increase what advantages he has.

Beyond that, it has always been fascinating to me that cheating is regarded as the cardinal sin of baseball. In comparison, acts of physical and sexual violence historically don't rank at all, given how poor Major League Baseball's record has been in dealing with those particular infractions in the past. Thanks to examples like the Black Sox scandal (where the Chicago White Sox were paid by gamblers to intentionally lose the 1919 World Series to the Cincinnati Reds) and the steroid era (a pre-crackdown period from the late eighties to the early-aughts, when steroid use was rampant before league-wide testing was implemented), cheating is an infraction that seems to induce more ire and league punishment than crimes that involve direct victims. (A recent example of this is Aroldis Chapman's thirty-game suspension for domestic violence, versus Colabello's eighty.) It's also a transgression that doesn't lend itself well to forgiveness from the sports community, and it will likely haunt Colabello long after his time has been served. In fact, TSN decided that "getting tangled up in PEDs could signal the death knell of his career," a point borne out by the fact that he didn't return to the Jays roster for the remainder of 2016. I've seen Alex Rodriguez, who served a full-season suspension for PEDs in 2014 and admitted to using steroids between 2001 and 2003, booed at enough games to understand that no one will be turning a blind eye to this, or writing the "coming back from a setback" narrative that is common with players who have committed actual crimes.

The disdain for cheating seems to go beyond ensuring basic policies of fairness and parity, and taps into what fans need to believe about the integrity of the sport in order to invest themselves fully in the game. When a player cheats, it reminds those who cheer from the stands that baseball is really more like theatre than they may want to believe. The act shakes our faith in the trustworthiness of what we're watching, and makes us replay earlier on-field moments with a sense of doubt or betrayal. (Rodriguez, for example, was voted the American League MVP during one of the years in which he later admitted to using steroids.) We have a hard time loving the game, and pouring our money into it, when we suspect the fantasy is tainted. And we're naturally emotional when we hear revelations of cheating, because we feel lied to by something we care deeply about. This is why the common response is to make an example of the offender, as a way to reaffirm the game's "innate goodness."

Colabello testing positive for PEDs was particularly painful because so many Jays fans were invested in the arduous, determined way he rose to baseball's main stage. By getting to the minors after seven long seasons playing independent ball, and making his major-league debut when he was just shy of thirty, he was someone fans could more easily identify with than the superhuman Mike Trouts and Bryce Harpers of the game. He's a player who (once) underscored the ideal that if you put in the effort, and were patient, you could one day achieve your goals. The fact that he might have taken PEDs explodes the mythology that hard work pays off, and upends the common belief that wanting something bad enough means you'll get it.

Further, Colabello is not an egomaniacal superstar popping pills to bask in a spotlight of false fame, glory, and excess; he clung to the outskirts of success, a classic underdog story that is much easier for someone in the stands to apply to their own life. Unlike someone like Rodriguez, if Colabello were taking PEDs he wasn't getting the extra help in order to be the very best, but instead to be "good enough" to stay in Major League Baseball.

In some ways I envy those with a knee-jerk response to Colabello's infraction. For fans ready to write him off, ready to scoff at his denial and his claims that he "spent every waking moment . . . trying to find an answer as to why or how," the news was not a complicated stew of feelings that need to be reckoned with. But for me and many others who cheered him on, processing the news of Colabello's suspension is an exercise in empathy that tests our notions about him, the game, and right and wrong. We are asked to decide whether or not we should believe a player we love, and to acknowledge there's absolutely no way we can ever know the truth. It turns out the theatre of baseball is not only about that precarious state of "fairness," but also about how little we really know these men we voluntarily root for, day in and day out.

I don't know Chris Colabello personally. Though everything I've heard about him suggests he's a "good person," I can't tell you whether or not he deliberately took drugs to enhance his performance. I can't tell you if his claim that he had no idea how his test came back positive is credible. What I can tell you is that good people make bad choices for a lot of different reasons, and sometimes that might even include cheating to stay in the game they love. The identity we projected onto Colabello is that he's a fighter who clawed his way onto one of the best teams in baseball, a precarious position that is likely rife with anxiety. If he did indeed make a decision to dope, there is certainly no way it should be condoned, but I do think there's little harm in making the effort to be empathetic.

Yes, maybe Colabello harmed the "integrity of the game." Maybe he shook our faith in him as a player. Maybe this was a kind of career death knell. But his actions were not so appalling that he doesn't deserve open-hearted forgiveness, or even the benefit of the doubt. Given everything the institution of baseball has taught us about cheating, that may not be the easiest response to have, but it certainly is the most compassionate.

"Just like the other teams that are in this battle are great, we are also great. It's about execution and coming in every day and not giving up—having that mentality that no matter what the score is you're always going to put up a fight. I believe we've done that. We showed that resilience and we've got to continue to do that, because that's what it's going to take."

JOSÉ BAUTISTA

"You have to plan and figure out where you're starting your slider and where it's going to end."

DAVID PRICE

"Whose candle are you going to light today?"

CHRIS ARCHER

on Twitter

"How can you expect everybody to be exactly the same? Act exactly the same? More importantly, why would you *want* them to?"

JOSÉ BAUTISTA

ALL ABOARD THE BANDWAGON

Toward the end of one of those dismal Blue Jays seasons, one rife with injury and disappointment, I brought a close friend of mine to her very first—and otherwise very poorly attended—baseball game at the Rogers Centre.

I perhaps get overly excited (and maybe even a little anxious) about being a part of someone's very first baseball outing. That's largely because I want them to love the game experience as much as I do, want them to enjoy every last minute of those nine innings—from the children's choir singing the national anthem, to the seventh-inning stretch, to the Herculean efforts of the closing pitcher.

General fandom was thin that season, but I'd been inviting a variety of unlikely enthusiasts—some of whom didn't know the rules, let alone the players' names—to join me in watching this game I adore. Many of them obliged simply because they loved me, and were happy to partake in something totally foreign to them if only because I spoke so enthusiastically about it. I admit I had a convincing and enticing shtick regarding the ballpark's myriad pleasures, and "when are we going to go to a game?" became a frequent refrain thanks to my inexpensive fan passes. This particular friend was one who enjoyed and wrote about football and UFC, and who had been kind enough to teach me the rules and the cast of characters of her chosen sports. I was more than happy to return the favour.

Whenever I take newbies to the ballpark, I kind of feel like I'm a hostess at what I believe is the world's best party, and that it's my job to make sure everyone in my company is having a really great time. I want a truly exciting game to play out in front of them—a win drenched in drama and Powerade, with myriad high and low points to act as an irresistible gateway drug for the previously uninitiated. Mostly, I want my companions to go through the rest of their lives dreamily telling the tale of the first time they were at what is indisputably my favourite place in the world.

If you've ever had the pleasure of introducing someone to live baseball, you'll know exactly what I'm talking about. It's wonderful to watch those first ballpark experiences through someone else's eyes, to see them get excited about all the things that many of us, so many games in, may take for granted. The hot dogs we're likely sick of having to eat because we consistently forget to have dinner before the game. The walk-up music we've heard so many times it's become background noise. The goofy giveaways and silly promo spots. The dramatic "around the league" montages on the video board and the endless mascot shenanigans. That hearty, seventh-inning singalong. Open-hearted newcomers are always thrilling seat companions, full of admirable, childlike giddiness and endless questions. With every new discovery, they remind you how complex and giving the game can actually be.

I still have a photo of my friend I took that day, somewhere around the fourth inning: a portrait of her reacting to seeing the Rogers Centre dome close when it started to rain. The structural marvel is something I've witnessed in action a number of times since I was ten years old, but watching it through her eyes made it new for me again. The look of awe and pure joy on her face was a great distillation of exactly why some of us revel in creating new baseball fans.

A few tall cans later, she gleefully dragged me from our 500-level nosebleeds to sneak down to some vacant seats behind home plate, an adventure made possible by her bravery and the fact that the Jays were, at the time, a pretty unpopular team. Once we were settled into our new vantage point, she hollered at plays and players like she'd been attending games for most of her life. She cheered. She booed. She light-heartedly heckled. She may not have always known what she was talking about, but she was having a really good time. I'd taken many people to see the Jays at this point, with varying degrees of success, but with her I'd done it. Frankly, I don't even remember if we won or lost, but for me it was a victory because *I'd made a baseball fan.*

Let's get something out of the way: there is absolutely nothing wrong with jumping on a sports-fandom bandwagon, and anyone who says otherwise hates joy.

The kind of people who regard new fans with disdain are nothing more than grown-up versions of the elementary schoolboys who wouldn't let you into their cool-kid clubhouse. Gatekeeping is never admirable, and what defines a "real fan" could possibly be one of the most boring topics of conversation in the world. (After people explaining their dreams.)

The reasonable among us lifelong adherents of the Church of Baseball know that it makes good sense to encourage as many devotees as possible. I'll even admit that my own personal mission to share the game with newcomers is a selfish one. Before I set out on a project of widespread initiation, my ballpark companions all looked very much the same—after my dad, my seatmate for more than thirty years and counting, they were always men in their twenties, many of whom had a very different experience of the game and its culture than I did. Though often well meaning, those men couldn't understand the inherent loneliness of being a female fan.

Sometimes when I meet a certain brand of baseball fan, I'm subjected to the typical name and stats-dropping test to prove my worthiness. *How long have you been a fan? How much do you actually know? How about that [insert obscure piece of baseball knowledge there is a good chance I've never heard of]?* Being a woman who loves the game often means I have to demonstrate that I'm not there simply to swoon over and crush on players, despite the fact that the hallmark of male coverage of women athletes is critiquing and slide-showing how they look in a bathing suit. All too often in the sports narrative, women are victims, accessories, girlfriends, or the person who brings you your beer. According to these dominant stereotypes, we're only pretending to like it, or just killing time at the park while the men enjoy the game. I'll never forget arriving in Florida for spring training for the first time in 2013, only to be met with a perplexed expression on the face of the guy in the rental car lineup when, in an otherwise casual, polite conversation between strangers, my husband clarified that no, he wasn't the baseball fan, I was.

Although baseball's female fan audience is significant, when I noticed that I wasn't meeting a lot of female fans in my day-to-day life, I had no choice but to make more. When you love a game whose culture doesn't love you back, it's only natural to try to recruit some much-needed support.

Call me paranoid, but it's hard for me not to see the subtext of the bandwagon conversation as gendered. Bandwagoning is an accusation often thrown at so-called fangirls, as if new, female voices will somehow sully or destroy all that is good about the game. It's a sentiment we've seen expressed in many communities where women have started to break down doors, whether it's in music, gaming, tech, literature, or art. Too often, male insiders shriek and whine that all will be ruined once the women arrive, rather than rightly celebrating the progressive evolution of the conversation.

It's so transparent, and it is, quite frankly, pathetic that some sport fans revel in excluding others just so they can feel like they solely control the way we talk about the game. I think it's absurd that anyone actually thinks an internationally played sport like baseball belongs exclusively to them, or that they have the right to play gatekeeper. Beyond that, I believe this hatred of newcomers is really about a fear of losing power, and reveals an anxiety around who gets to define sports culture and how it is discussed. This is not about the purity of the game experience, this is about a perceived loss of privilege.

I'm no longer interested in defending my right to fandom, nor in challenging the notion of my being "allowed" or "lucky enough" to talk about baseball. I don't want to have to constantly prove my worthiness by counting up how many years I've invested in the sport, or by showing the volume of knowledge I have. That's a trap, a fool's game, lending itself to schoolyard-style tussles and childish shouting matches.

I will, however, say this: I have never felt more comfortable being a baseball fan than I have in the last couple of years. The recent growth of my team's bandwagon has created the necessary room—not only for me, but for so many others—to be part of this community. Though newbies are so often derided, we should really be grateful to see them. Their arrival is evidence that the larger baseball community is flourishing, and that everyone is welcome to be a part of it.

People who rail against bandwagoners are usually those who have, for far too long, held the sole power to dictate the culture around the sport. They are perfectly content to yell "get off my lawn, poser!" without examining the real value brought by those who don't fit their image of what a fan should be. For the rest of us, men and women alike, who are enthused to see a new diversity of voices and perspectives populating the way we discuss sports, we'll continue our recruitment.

While those on the inside like to keep their numbers small, those on the outside will take all the help they can get to push the door wide open.

During the 2016 Jays season, with its average game-day stadium attendance up a whopping 10,000 over the year I took my friend to see her very first game, I ran into her in a lengthy beer lineup on the concourse. She was clutching a foot-long hotdog drenched in mustard, and had donned a baseball cap tilted sideways. After a hug, she let me know she'd come to the park that day with a large group of people, most of whom had never seen a game in person before.

She was passing the torch, filling up her own personal bandwagon, and I couldn't have been happier.

There is real pleasure to be had in sharing the thing you care about with those who could potentially feel the same way you do. The idea that people who celebrate sports are inviting more fans on board is one that fills me with optimism, not some strange, greedy, covetous dismay. It's the same satisfaction you get when you lend out your favourite album or book, and it's returned with shared appreciation and infatuation.

What you've done is to help someone fall in love.

A SHAMEFUL CODE OF RETRIBUTION

The game of baseball is defined by being a "non-contact" sport, its rules dictating that players barely touch each other, a fact that only becomes truer with time. (For the past few years, the MLB powers that be have tried to reduce the risk of bodies violently crashing into each other by instituting a new slide rule and measures to avoid leg-breaking home-plate collisions.) Baseball actively looks to avoid the brutal blows and body checks of the hockey rink, and doesn't have the same concussion epidemic as its NFL counterpart. In fact, so many fans I know come to this game precisely for that reason—because it doesn't evoke injurious combat, or cash in on gratuitous damage.

This is why when violence does occur in baseball, whether executed on the field or off, it always feels jarring. When Chase Utley breaks Rubén Tejada's leg with a hard slide into second, or Jonathan Papelbon chokes Bryce Harper in the dugout, or an on-field brawl breaks out at Globe Life Park between the Texas Rangers and the Toronto Blue Jays, we (should) generally feel uncomfortable and unnerved by the whole thing. That's not why we're here, we think. This is supposed to be a slow, meandering, civilized game. We're supposed to exist and cheer under the illusion of widespread gentlemanliness.

I certainly won't claim that baseball fans are universally a bunch of empathetic pacifists (you only need to look at my Twitter mentions to dispute that naive idea), but explicit direct hits, like the one we saw the Texas Rangers' Rougned Odor give José Bautista during the eighth inning of the final game of the teams' May 2016 series, always feel alien in a game predicated on players only ever lightly touching each other. Sure, they get emotional, they get "hotheaded," but they don't come to *Road House*–style blows, right? "The Game" is better than that, right? It's elegant, and intelligent, and above all that, right?

Yet this illusion of the sport being a gentleman's game conceals an undercurrent of retribution that is coded into baseball itself. There are all those pesky unwritten rules that we keep hearing about—dictums that demand you act a certain way lest you get plunked with a fastball, or skewered with an aggressive slide. These are the same "rules" that lead people to think of recently banned sexist hazing rituals as hilarious, that require rookies to wear little girls' backpacks and always know their place, that endorse upstarts getting "appropriately" shamed, and that ensure Bautista's celebratory bat flip gets the payback it "deserved." These rules are damaging and distracting, and during that Jays–Rangers game, they caused players' feelings to boil over, culminating in an ugly discordant punch to José Bautista's face that was played on a gleeful slo-mo loop by anyone who subscribes to this kind of archaic thinking.

If you were contrarian enough to have an anti-violence stance during that game, or brave enough to say that no one scuffling was in the right (except maybe Adrian Beltre, with his violence-diffusing Bautista bear hug), you were told repeatedly that you don't understand how baseball works. It's a game of revenge, apparently. One where, seven months after an emotionally fraught playoff game, a team can get theirs and it's considered entirely appropriate. And if you stared in disbelief as a group of men you admire brutalized one another in a frenzied pit of hostility—again, you just don't understand how baseball works, and should probably just look away.

"Because he flipped his bat, Bautista got what he deserved," "Bautista was asking for it," "Bautista needs to take it like a man, hashtag karma"—this was the general pro-plunking and pro-punching stance. (Pretty sure that's not the intended interpretation of the word *karma*, but okay, whatever bros.) Some of the brilliant minds on social media even went as far as to claim that this was a good lesson for children: *Don't be openly proud of your accomplishments lest ye get hit in the ribs and punched squarely in the jaw, little one.*

What kind of deranged, destructive viewpoint is that?

When baseball disputes happen, we're expected to take a side—brand one team or player evil, the other good, and then fight it out viciously among the fanbases. We fail to foster any productive dialogue or nuance, nor do we understand how ingrained systems of institutional violence just beget more violence, and that a "pound of flesh" pitch is a sanctioned first step toward a punch in the face. We watch as high-profile commentators like Sportsnet's Gregg Zaun trot out their hallowed old-school baseball ideals, claiming that this is just the way it is, the way it's supposed to be, and everyone involved is simply a puppet in baseball's grand, mythical stage play.

"I'm here to tell you that in this whole situation everybody did as they were supposed to do," said Zaun post-game, following up with numerous additional "supposed to's" to drive his entirely weak point home.

Zaun suggests that if you're "squeamish" you should just look away, but I take great offence to that, just like I take offence to the idea that I don't enjoy baseball violence simply because I don't get it. This is my game as much as it is the game of those who view it through Zaun's fetishized, old-school lens. I am allowed to object to escalating (and sometimes illegal) aggressive acts, sanctioned or otherwise, and to suggest that there's got to be another, better way to play. The fact is, when violence is promoted as an appropriate dispute resolution in sports, that concept can bleed into all areas of our lives, with dire results.

Frankly, I'm tired of hearing about the need to "man up" and "settle scores" as an excuse for egregious behaviour. I'm tired of literal assault being excused in a game context. I came to baseball fandom precisely because it offered me a shelter from the ubiquity of violence, and I am allowed to express my disappointment when aggression rears its ugly head in this place where I've found refuge. When people talk about what a terrible example Bautista set via his celebratory gesture, or how bad a role model full-of-himself Bryce Harper is, I have to wonder why encouraging this kind of punishing, vengeful masculinity is somehow the better option. Why hitting people with pitches, slides, and fists is what is "supposed to happen."

Though our animal brains are likely thrilled by the drama that went down in Texas, our honed reason should always default to "violence, in whatever form, is a problem." That means everyone involved had a part in that toxic stew, from Matt Bush hitting Bautista with a pitch, to Jesse Chavez returning the favour with Prince Fielder, to Bautista's aggressive slide, to Odor's merciless punch. As hard as it is to admit, even Kevin Pillar and Josh Donaldson, with their steadfast if bulldozing "support your teammate" reactions, were in the wrong. And despite some fan admiration, hearing Pillar invoke eye for an eye and militaristic language in a scrum postgame didn't make me think he was commendable. Just because someone did something worse doesn't make what you did any better. I can certainly empathize that they're men in the moment, that emotions are at eleven, and that loyalty is important, but someone at some point has to make a choice to stop the momentum of violence.

Though the theatre of it all understandably entertains and amuses, it shouldn't be remotely controversial to suggest that every plot point in the narrative that played out that day is worthy of our critique. We shouldn't be jubilantly comparing this to "great base-brawls and punches in sports history," or calling people heroes because they decided to join in the spat. Regardless of our affiliations, it was a nasty scene all around, and if you don't think so, you're just using baseball to condone hurting another human being.

You can do the mental gymnastics. You can tie yourself in knots trying to figure out who started it, who was asking for what, and who gets anointed with the label of "The Worst." But in the end, the side of right is always going to be: *Don't punch a guy in the face because of a game.*

If you take offence to that, maybe you just don't understand baseball.

ON GOING TO THE BALLPARK ALONE

On a Saturday afternoon in May 2016, I went to a baseball game by myself. I bought a single aisle seat in section 233 at Yankee Stadium, and took the D train from Manhattan to the Bronx alone. I dutifully followed strangers in Yankees caps to make sure I didn't get lost, and then grabbed my own at the team store as a strategy to blend in with the hordes. I took the escalator up to my level, purchased a beer in a plastic souvenir cup, and, during an unseasonably chilly three hours, watched the Yanks beat former Blue Jay David Price, and the rest of the Boston Red Sox, 8–2. It was in so many ways a perfect day, and one I desperately needed.

At least once a season, I try to fit in a solo pilgrimage to the ballpark, just like that afternoon of solitude in New York. I've been gifted a single front-row seat on the third-base line at the Rogers Centre and enjoyed the presence of the friendly season-ticketed lonely hearts seated around me—some chose to strike up a conversation with a stranger, while others remained glued to the headphone-assisted privacy of their in-game radio broadcasts. One year during spring training, I stationed myself directly behind home plate at Joker Marchant Stadium in Lakeland, Florida, where I spent a relaxing afternoon quietly watching Detroit Tigers pitcher Justin Verlander lead his team to victory. I spoke to no one besides the kindly beer vendor, and took a fifth-inning opportunity to sprawl out by myself on a grassy berm.

The experience reminds me that solitude among the buzz of a busy stadium is like a kind of meditation. Even when there are thousands of people around, it's really just you, your thoughts, your favourite pitcher, and the nine men in your lineup.

Baseball is an incredibly social sport to love. It's a game that attracts a vast community of fans to buoy you through wins and losses, good times and bad. Sometimes I even measure my affection for baseball in the many connections I've made, and the community I've fostered through it. In the digital age, baseball is a game you can watch with countless others without ever leaving your couch, with each play celebrated or lamented via shared online musings. I often find myself forming my in-game reactions from that cacophony of voices, and I value the experience because it pulls me out of my solitude and into the world.

For those of us who are introverted, baseball provides a comfortable space to talk about something outside ourselves. When people discover you love the game, it can replace the usual chit-chat about work and relationships. The excitement, joy, and devastation that baseball provides means you're never short of things to talk about, especially when you want to steer the conversation away from things you'd prefer not to discuss.

Baseball can also be a good facilitator for those times when you need to talk about what's really important. Ever since my dad was my first seatmate, the ballpark has been a safe place for me to confide my thoughts and confess my deep dark secrets to friends old and new. The graceful (and yes, at times excruciatingly slow) pace of nine innings makes it easy to pay attention to both the sporadic action and the person by your side. Further, there's something about sitting next to someone—as opposed to across from them—that makes it easier for those who struggle with their feelings to share them. Watching a ball game creates the same sort of conversational ease as taking a long road trip with a beloved companion, with the bonus of a freshly grilled hot dog and intermittent on-field entertainment.

But, in the spirit of good baseball life advice, and at the risk of treading too far into metaphor, sometimes you just have to take the D train to the Bronx and go to the game on your own. Sometimes you have to strip away all the other voices in the conversation, and just listen to yourself for a while.

In September 2015, I left my magazine marketing job of seven years and pursued writing—about the game of baseball and other things—full-time. It was a scary yet necessary decision, though one that I recognize the inherent privilege of being able to make at all. Leaving the security of a steady paycheque and the bonus of health insurance meant a lot of emotional buildup and a great deal of saving for the financially insecure days that were sure to come. While I may have thoroughly prepared myself in all of the important logistical ways—the contents of my bank account made me relatively comfortable, and I had a few reliable freelance writing gigs and a solid backup plan in place—I don't think I was cognizant of what can happen when you become untethered from the daily socializing that comes along with a traditional full-time job.

When I finally packed up my desk, the Toronto Blue Jays were in the midst of gunning for their first postseason presence in over twenty years, clinching the American League East in the first few weeks of my new, self-imposed exile from the regular working world. While I was enthusiastically cheering them on, I was also realizing that I had long forgotten the fine art of being alone (if I had ever really learned it in the first place), and finding that one of the only times I was around other people now was when I was at the ballpark. The daily quiet and the inevitable loneliness hit me hard during what was already a time of uncertainty. Suddenly, the lifeline that the ballpark and the baseball community had always offered became all the more vital.

Showing up at an office from nine to five, and then going home to eat dinner with your partner, means there's little time to face who you are, or even to hear yourself think. Now that every one of my workdays requires at least eight hours of being completely by myself, I've had to relearn that skill of solitude, to admittedly mixed results. Some days, I'm optimistic and think I've really come into my own voice as a result of that ever-present quiet. Other days, I worry that I'm descending into a kind of anxious, shut-in void that makes me reluctant to put on pants and go to a social event.

What the experience has taught me is how often we measure our skills and our talents—and understand our beliefs—relationally and competitively, and how in doing so we ignore who we are and what we really want. We habitually compare ourselves to others to a debilitating degree, believing our successes can only be captured by how much we've outpaced someone else. We deal in acceptable ideas. We disregard our own capabilities. We waste a lot of time and emotion on what everyone else is doing well or badly, when we should be investing in and celebrating ourselves. And sometimes we simply forget that we like our own company, or that we love things for our own, deeply personal, individualistic reasons.

In short, we forget ourselves, and how to be alone.

It was for this reason that trip to Yankee Stadium, eight months after making the jump to terrifying freedom, felt particularly meaningful. Of course, if you love baseball and you happen to be in New York, going to see the Yankees face the Red Sox is exactly what you should do, regardless of whether or not you have someone to go with. The historic rivalry has an innate thrill to it, and is much more jovial and warm-hearted than the legend would suggest. The mass booing of retirement-bound David Ortiz was oddly light and comical, and a Yankees fan and a Sox fan in front of me in the beer line had a good laugh about the absurdity of it all. It was a joy to chat with complete strangers, to talk ball with people of varying allegiances, and to dictate my own schedule of when it was time to sit and when it was time to wander. I didn't have to explain or listen to an explanation of a play, or say a single word. I even went ahead and sang "Take Me Out to the Ball Game" at full volume without reservation or embarrassment—simultaneously solo and in a beautiful, jubilant choir of thousands.

But I also think I bought a single ticket because I needed to fully embrace the quiet, and have it just be the game and me for a little while. Amid the ambient sounds of the stadium, the ump's calls and the smacking of ball to glove, I needed to remind myself that yes, I am capable, and that yes, my love for baseball (and the love I get back from it) is not predicated on any interaction or external validation. Sure, the game is undeniably a community endeavour, but your love for it can only deepen when you take the time to realize what you alone bring to all its tiny dramas, losses, and victories. You can better appreciate its meditative effect, its rich solace, when it's just you, and the game, and a Blue Moon Belgian White in your Yankees souvenir cup.

Over the last year I've faced a great deal of uncertainty and doubt. I've been scared and anxious, worried about what I'm doing, why I'm doing it, and where it all will take me. I've felt unsure, and perhaps I've made the mistake of looking outside myself, and of comparing myself to others, to find the answers. If only for an afternoon, I needed to go ahead and buy a single ticket and remind myself that maybe I already have all the answers I need.

And as always, the ballpark generously reassured me. Baseball, it said, means you're never alone, but it also teaches you that it's okay to be all by yourself.

"There's always somebody out there that's going to probably be better than you. There's always somebody out there that's probably going to be outworking you. What are you going to do to be better? You're going to have to put in the time."

LISA FRENCH

(Josh Donaldson's mom)

"I've forgiven him but I don't think you ever forget. The fact of the matter is you can't go back and change what you did yesterday. You hope that people learn from it. You hope it makes them a better human being."

JOSH DONALDSON

on his father and the domestic abuse he witnessed as a child

"This isn't the 'try league.' This is the 'get-it-done league.'"

JOSH DONALDSON

OUR CHARMING DIRTBAG BOYFRIEND

Baseball can be, in more ways than one, an optimal training ground for dealing with loss. You have incredibly strong feelings about a team and then, all of a sudden, pieces of it disappear into the abyss. At the trade deadline or in the offseason, your beloved heroes are sent away to Detroit, or Milwaukee, or Oakland, or Boston. The game generously teaches you that even though you feel that sad, tearful heartbreak over losing one of your favourites, perhaps the player you're getting in return might be worth all the pain of saying goodbye.

A player, for example, like Joshua Adam Donaldson.

I will readily admit I was a little wary when Josh Donaldson joined the Toronto Blue Jays from the Oakland Athletics in November 2014. During his first spring training in Dunedin, my eye was so focused on fellow newcomer Russell Martin that I can't remember seeing Donaldson there at all. (In retrospect, shame on me.) In baseball conversations, I jokingly referred to the third baseman as "new Dad," revealing my reluctance to embrace him as part of my baseball family after losing some players I adored. To me he was an unknown, and while many tried to convince me that the acquisition was a good one, I'm a person who revels in the comfort of the familiar.

The first thing that made me take notice of Donaldson was not actually his performance on the field, but rather how much his haircut reminded me of a boyfriend I had back in junior high during the 1990s. After watching some long shots of the dugout during a game, I suddenly noticed he had this undeniable, crush-worthy boy-band quality, at once recognizable and mysterious, like that quiet guy in your English class whose name you wrote out in ballpoint pen on the inside of your backpack when you were thirteen. While the baseball insiders were throwing around cold stats and predictions about who he would be on the field, I was building a narrative about the handsome new face on our bench.

And then, during a game on May 18, 2015, Josh Donaldson told the Angels bench to "suck my cock." The moment was soundlessly captured on camera, and if I'm perfectly honest, that's when the fan love affair began for me. (By the way, after said comment, the Blue Jays went on to win that game 10–6.) Objectively, what an odd, unlikely, and perhaps personally incongruous reason to be drawn to a player. I've never been a real fan of hurling machismo insults, but I was totally enthralled by his strange breed of slick bravado and brassiness. I was mesmerized by the way he took no shit and yet still seemed like the kind of guy who would show up for the team when you needed him to.

In August 2015, I shared a missive on social media: "Josh Donaldson is your guy friend and you're having a beer at the bar together and some guy says some bullshit to you and Josh intervenes." Donaldson was so compelling as a player that Toronto fans who followed me added to a growing list of things they imagined Donaldson could do for you as a friend and confidant:

"Josh Donaldson comes and changes a flat when you're stranded on the side of the road."

"Josh Donaldson always makes sure everyone gets home safe from the bar."

"Josh Donaldson reaches an arm across you protectively when he brakes hard, even though you're wearing a seatbelt."

"Josh Donaldson lets you take the last slice of pizza."

As a woman wary of self-anointed "nice guys," Donaldson is in so many ways the perfect baseball crush. He's enigmatic and alluring, but also refreshingly easygoing and transparent. What you see is what you get, and what you get is amusingly perplexing: a casual smirk, an eyebrow raised, an innuendo or two, a delightful grin. A considered yet unselfconscious fiery swagger doused in a bucket full o' Powerade. He's the goofball, and the guy with the blaring speaker in his hip pocket at spring training. Someone who is both performing in a considered way and completely, genuinely himself—aware of the cameras being on him but not seeming to care all that much that they're there. A strong, silent type who's also totally in your face, telling the opposing bench to suck his cock. Someone who smiles at his own home runs and laughs at his own jokes. The sweetly shy bad boy who loves and supports the tough-as-nails single mom who raised him. In fact, I think there are many fans who would admit to shedding a tear when, after he was inevitably named the American League's Most Valuable Player in 2015, the first thing he did was turn to his mom and say, "We won."

I'm not sure at what point I nicknamed Donaldson our "charming dirtbag boyfriend," but those words seemed to accurately sum up his inexplicable charisma. Fans have noted he's reminiscent of such captivating characters as John Bender from *The Breakfast Club* or Tim Riggins from television's *Friday Night Lights*—sure, maybe a little unpredictable and rough around the edges, but fundamentally warm and loyal when it matters. The dirtbag is what makes him a rough-and-tumble, no-holds-barred player, and the charm is what allows him to transcend team allegiances to win league-wide fan acclaim. (For the record, I once asked Donaldson how he felt about being anointed with that title, and like a true charming dirtbag he said, "I'm okay with it.")

For so many, Josh Donaldson gave us permission to admit to being attracted to baseball players, and allowed those otherwise uninterested in the game to get on board a bandwagon of appreciative feelings. I mean, he could do something as simple as put on a blazer or a pair of calf-accentuating pants, or sport a new hairstyle, and the entire Internet would explode. Further, he had a way of modelling a Roots jacket in a promo spot that suggested "viewer discretion is advised."

The more people I discuss this vital, pressing baseball issue with, the more I realize that Josh Donaldson taps into a sort of attraction that we find difficult to parse. On the surface he's a typical (though incredibly skilled) jock, with his mouth often enthusiastically agape and his tongue expressively hanging out, a hearty "fuck you" being one of his stock critical phrases. He's all ego and brash behaviour, and yet for a certain demographic he induces a nostalgic desire reminiscent of our teenage years, when we wore cherry Lip Smackers and fumble-kissed boys with shaved bowl haircuts. As I've mentioned, the culture of baseball fandom doesn't exactly sanction the discussion of physical attraction to players, making it all the more difficult to unpack his cryptic magnetism. We're forced to speak in hushed whispers and euphemisms, struggling to comprehend why a guy who made a hand gesture to his genitals on camera would set our hearts aflame. (You got theories? I'm all ears.)

The thing is, even with all his evident blue-eyed heartthrob qualities, his winning smile, and undeniably cocky yet paradoxically humble swagger, Josh Donaldson is also really, really good at The Game. Before that hallowed ALDS game happened, Donaldson gave Jays fans what was arguably one of the most blisteringly emotional baseball moments of 2015—a walk-off home run to end the last homestand of the season—before gifting us a series of photos of him in a now famous, Powerade-drenched black tank top that will remain forever saved on the phones of his admirers everywhere. He's a player who can hover-slide safely into home plate, receive the most All-Star votes of all time, and, when that MVP conversation rumbled, be gracious every time the media questioned him about it.

At the risk of turning this into a big "remember the time when?" party, he was even captured in-game on camera, snuggling his bat longingly, exactly like that sensitive bad boy from our teen years, leaning up against his locker with a faraway look in his eye.

Experts have said that Josh Donaldson plays baseball like a football player, and that he performs with a "look at me" quality that alarms those who just want to see him stay healthy. "I'm not saying I want it about me," he told *60 Minutes*, "but at the same time I'm gonna go out there and let you know that I'm on the field." He's indeed very physical, dramatically throwing his whole body into every play, yet Donaldson is an athlete of multiple graceful paradoxes. With all his hulking physical power, he still manages to resemble a dancer on the field, ever nimble and light-footed. He is somehow both aggressive and delicate, taking up his deserved space yet consistently sacrificing himself to a play. He's equal parts bombastic impetuousness, and measured, considered, thoughtful technique. It's all emotive science. Feelings meet logic, if you will.

Donaldson is a messy player, and how he achieved his elite baseball status is a messy story. In high school he played football, basketball, and baseball, and ended up as a catcher and third baseman at Auburn University. The Chicago Cubs drafted him in 2007, and he made his major-league debut against the Blue Jays as an Oakland Athletic a few years later. He readily admits that, early in his MLB career, he wasn't much of a player to write home about, his struggles at the plate sending him back and forth from the majors to the minors. "I looked up and I saw Barry Zito's batting average, and I was like, jeez, their pitcher's hitting better than me," he recalled in that same *60 Minutes* interview. It wasn't until 2013 that Donaldson really hit his stride, evolving into the kind of athlete that the Toronto Blue Jays would deem worthy of acquiring by trade in the offseason.

But Donaldson's reputation as someone who has overcome adversity goes deeper than what he's accomplished on the field. He grew up in an environment of domestic violence (his father served fifteen years in prison for crimes committed against Donaldson's mother and others), and has become a sort of unassuming patron saint for the genuinely hard done by, those who have seen the worst but have managed to rise to greatness nonetheless. "The past is the past," he has said, and anyone who has come through life's hardships understands the necessity of the sentiment. The very idea that he witnessed tragedy, was taunted by teammates in high school, yet evolved into a self-assured superstar, is a mind-blowing, inspiring, and even consoling example to follow.

It's no secret that Donaldson has been the purveyor of so many riveting baseball moments during his brief time as a Toronto Blue Jay. He was responsible for what might have been the most mind-bending catch of 2015, one that had him diving over a few rows in the stands and almost crushing a small child to make the out. He is known for coming into a base with a dramatic hair flip and victorious gesture, and can destroy a baseball with the best of them, recording a whopping 41 home runs and 123 RBIs during the 2015 season.

In August 2016, during a Rogers Centre–hosted game against the Minnesota Twins, he hit three home runs in eight innings, a feat that prompted fans to throw their caps onto the field to celebrate his hat trick. (As a souvenir, Donaldson ended up carrying two large garbage bags packed with those hats out of the ballpark that day.)

And in the final moments of the 2016 American League Division Series, Donaldson was the game-winning hero who hustled to home on Texas Ranger Rougned Odor's throwing error. When he cleared home plate, he threw one arm dramatically in the air and ran straight into the open arms of teammate Troy Tulowitzki. With that aggressive sprint, the Jays swept the Rangers, and were on their way to the league championship series for the second year in a row.

Donaldson has been a key, high-profile figure in so many of my beloved baseball memories, but perhaps my favourite has less to do with his on-field performance and more to do with what he really means to the fans who cheer for him. In July 2015, I had the opportunity to see the third baseman play in Oakland for the first time since he was traded to the Jays. That day, A's fans wore their old Donaldson jerseys with pride, and gave him an unrestrained standing ovation during his first at-bat.

When I wandered the concourse of Oakland Coliseum that afternoon, a very sweet woman spotted my Blue Jays jersey and stopped me to chat. She wanted to let me know how lucky we were to have Donaldson on our team, and would we please "take care of him" for her.

It was incredibly moving to see a fanbase embrace a former player that way, with their handmade signs and the spontaneous yelling of "we love you, Josh!" (He tipped his cap and mouthed the words "thank you" to that like a perfect gentleman.) And it was heartbreaking, too, to watch them endure the same loss of a player that had induced my own wariness at the beginning of the season.

It is true that we often know so little about the players we come to love. We are rarely privy to their belief systems, or the way they treat the people in their lives. But we form a connection to athletes in much the same way we come to adore the characters in our favourite books. We revel in the feelings they conjure, and enjoy what our love for them reveals about ourselves.

Though it may feel odd to be so proud of the achievements of someone we barely know, who wouldn't want success for a player who has done so many near-impossible things on the field? But more than that, maybe it's really the *idea* of Josh Donaldson that we love so much, and the way that idea has brought all of us "charming dirtbags" together. His rise to success reminds us that you have to make sure what other people have done to you doesn't drag you down. You have to work hard and get back up when you fall. You have to always keep moving forward. And sometimes you have to get a little dirty to get the job done.

MORE THAN MEAN

> "Aristotle defined human beings as language-using creatures. They are not always as well-behaved as wolves, but everything humane depends on words—love, promise-keeping, story-telling, democracy. And baseball."
>
> *Washington Post journalist* GEORGE F. WILL
> *on the retirement of beloved Dodgers announcer, Vin Scully*

In 2016, sports reporter and friend Julie DiCaro (along with espnW columnist Sarah Spain) appeared in a public service announcement titled #MoreThanMean, where men were asked to read out loud—to her—actual online messages she received while doing her job. DiCaro is an update anchor for Chicago's 670 The Score and a writer who often focuses on the intersection of sports culture and violence against women. As a result, she's on the receiving end of a great deal of abuse. In fact, the first time I ever heard about DiCaro was when a colleague described her as "that woman sportswriter who gets threatened with rape all the time." Her coverage of the sexual assault allegations against Chicago Blackhawk Patrick Kane garnered responses so vitriolic—she received death threats, with one online commentator posting a photograph of the side door she uses to get into her workplace—that there were times she chose not to go to her job out of a genuine concern for her safety.

The reason the video is so affecting is because of the palpable discomfort the men reveal when they're forced to read, to DiCaro's face, tweets like "One of the players should beat you to death with their hockey stick like the whore you are," "Cunt," and "I hope you get raped again." The men repeatedly ask if they really have to say these things, and apologize profusely when they do. It's a sad commentary that, even though women have been talking and writing about online abuse for years, it takes men showing us how this kind of abuse affects *them* negatively for it to be taken seriously. But the PSA certainly did its job. At the time of writing, the video has been watched more than 3.8 million times on YouTube.

Although Julie DiCaro's experience is on the extreme end of online harassment, her story resonates with many women who talk about sports, regardless of whether they're high-profile columnists or simply fans trying to be part of a larger community.

I started writing about baseball in 2011 because I assumed it would be a safer, happier realm to work in. At the time, a lot of my work dealt with topics of sexual assault, sexism, and abuse in a non–sports related context, and I was experiencing a lot of emotional fatigue as a result. Since watching baseball has always been a comfort to me, and the ballpark a place I can go that offers both fun and distraction, I naturally thought writing about the game would give me the same relief. Though it certainly has been rewarding, and I am grateful for all the opportunities I've been given, I couldn't have been more wrong. In retrospect, it turns out it's naive to assume that "safety" and "happiness" are what women get when they share their opinions about sports in a public way.

When *Sports Illustrated* ran a link to a rather innocuous tweet I wrote after Jays manager John Gibbons made some sexist postgame comments ("Maybe we'll come out wearing dresses tomorrow. Maybe that's what everyone is looking for."), I received unsolicited messages for days telling me how stupid and wrong I was, as well as an invitation to "come see my nudes." I understand it's within anyone's right to disagree with me, but an onslaught of critical tweets from complete strangers doesn't exactly foster intelligent discourse. There's also a distinction between having a differing opinion and just gleefully hurling online abuse.

When I briefly mentioned the same Gibbons incident in a positive piece on recent progress made by Major League Baseball on gender equity and LGBT issues, a vast majority of the sixty-seven commenters told me to "lighten up" and "get a life," and that I was "sucky and whiny." They made accusations of ranting political correctness and McCarthyism. One particularly articulate commenter offered, "Blah blah blah blah sexism, blah blah blah blah racism, blah blah blah blah pay equity." Another piece I wrote on baseball hazing garnered comments as predictable as "relax ladies quit whining," and as out of left field as "offensive women journalists invading the privacy of men's locker rooms in baseball." Once, when I deliberately ignored the comments for the sake of my mental health, one man took it upon himself to find me on Twitter and excitedly tell me how terrible they were.

Now, of course, the examples I've mentioned here are not as serious as the rape and death threats that DiCaro endures almost daily, but should I really be grateful that when I publish a piece, dozens of strangers feel the need to insult my beliefs and my intelligence? Should I actually be thankful that today someone only posted a comment that I was a hack, or that I write like "a middle school English student"? And, really, what incentive does anyone have to continue writing about sports at all, if those are the comments they have to look forward to every time they publish? (On my more cynical days, it just feels like women sportswriters are sacrificing their well-being for the good of corporate rage clicks.)

The direct abuse may be the worst of it, but the pervasive climate of inevitable cruelty conjures a nagging fear every time I write something or simply have an opinion in a public forum. I've lost the excitement I once felt whenever my baseball writing was about to be published. In its place is a fog of anxiety and dread, the compulsion to second-guess myself, and the need to read and reread my work over and over to ensure there's nothing that will provide fodder for someone to attack me relentlessly. Some of my editors have even done "troll reads," weeding out lines in my pieces that run the risk of being a honeypot for a swarm of jerks, while others have disabled comments on articles that deal with sensitive topics like domestic violence and sexual assault. If I *am* brave enough to have a progressive sports opinion publicly that I know will inflame the masses, I now hold my breath and prepare myself for the inevitable attack to follow.

That's no way to work and earn a living—and no way to live—no matter how many times people insist the cruelty is "just the reality of the Internet" and that you should either suck it up, or hide away and find something else to do. Even if you've never been harassed personally, witnessing what women like DiCaro go through understandably discourages you from putting yourself and your opinions out there, which only further perpetuates the terrible gender imbalance in the sports conversation.

Some critics of DiCaro's PSA argued that male sportswriters and personalities also attract insults, harassment, and abuse, and I don't deny that is true. Sports culture definitely has a toxic undercurrent that belies the "it's just a game" surface, and we're all swimming in it daily. But it seems to me that men are driving a great deal of that toxicity, and that gendered insults have the very real effect of further excluding women from a realm where they've been repeatedly told they don't belong. I admit I've had crisis moments when I'm not sure if I want to do this work anymore, not sure if I can endure the trade-off between my mental health and my ability to make a living. I've even scaled back on expressing my opinions on social media to deter abuse. That's a horrible, exhausting reality given how hard I—and so many other women—have worked just to make our voices heard in this male-dominated conversation.

The thing that saddens me the most when it comes to discussions about online viciousness is how futile they feel. Every so often a video is made, or an essay is written, and we talk about how awful everything is—but nothing really changes. In fact, things only seem to get worse. (In a truly "gross, but of course" moment, DiCaro faced a great deal of harassment for simply *talking about harassment*. In the days after the PSA was released, her Twitter account was once again flooded with all manner of cruelty.) For me, it's gotten to the point where I wake up in the morning and immediately check social media to make sure someone isn't being creepy, threatening, or unkind. People tell us not to read the comments, not to feed the trolls, and to block, block, block, but none of that addresses the threat to our livelihoods or the real psychological harm that this steady stream of hatred instills. In fact, a recent conversation I had with a few women in sports media revealed that they, like me, are actually afraid to ignore and block the worst offenders, as doing so tends to escalate the situation and makes abusers more obsessive and more intent on recruiting others to assist in their campaign.

So how exactly do we make things better? While I'm sure most of us would agree threatening a woman with rape and murder is wrong, we need to acknowledge that there are lesser forms of abuse that masquerade as a simple difference of opinion. Feel free to disagree with someone's opinion, but also assess whether the way you publicly share that disagreement forwards the conversation and sheds light on an issue, or if it's nothing but harmful. Adding your personal "this is fucking stupid" to dozens of other similar comments doesn't create dialogue or understanding, but instead makes another person feel like garbage.

I hate that online harassment has tainted the enthusiasm I once had for being part of the sports community, and for writing about the game and the team I love. I hate that it fills me with fear and doubt, and makes me question whether I should even bother. I hate that the days when I'm unsure if this is even a healthy space for me are becoming more frequent, and that I can feel myself pulling away from writing about important topics because I know they'll just attract abuse.

Most of all, I hate that to be successful—or even visible—you are told you have to toughen up and "take it."

I don't want to end on Golden Rule platitudes, or warm and fuzzy calls for empathy. That kind of talk feels inadequate in the face of how intent some people are on demoralizing and destroying others. I do, however, want readers to understand that this abuse, in its many forms, resonates long after a single comment or tweet is read. Online vitriol is silencing vital ideas and discourse, and it will continue to cause harm long after the attention the #MoreThanMean PSA has rightfully garnered dies down.

Beyond thinking and saying online abuse is wrong, you should support those who endure it—not only in the interest of being compassionate, but to ensure a better, safer, and more robust sports community for everyone.

FATHER'S DAY AT THE BALLPARK

I remember the exact moment when my dad sat down with me and explained how a player's batting average is calculated. I was just a kid at the time, my love of baseball in its earliest, uninformed stages. He patiently walked me through all those weird numbers next to my favourite sluggers' names, going over the simple stats in a way that was easy for a child to understand.

"So if a batter comes up to the plate ten times . . ."

In retrospect, my dad was probably still learning about how baseball works himself. As a British transplant who immigrated to Canada in 1977—incidentally, the same year the Blue Jays played their first matchup at Exhibition Stadium—he started going to the ballpark as a way to understand his new North American home. Given my mother's relative indifference toward the game, I was my father's default stadium companion from the time I was still in diapers. As he became enthralled with the sport, he shared his increasing wisdom with me until I was old enough to read the rule book for myself.

I know it's stereotypical and clichéd, but it's nearly impossible for me to watch Father's Day go by each year without thinking about how my love of baseball was nurtured by my dad. He was my very first teacher and seatmate at the ballpark—beginning on those shiny silver bleachers at Exhibition, with their haphazardly spray-painted black numbers, and then at the newly minted SkyDome, with its then awe-inspiring amenities. (When the building officially opened in June 1989, we marvelled at its five restaurants, the in-stadium hotel, what was at the time the biggest video board in the world, and, of course, the revolutionary retractable, rotatable dome roof.)

When I became an adolescent, my dad was the reason I got to see the Blue Jays through exciting playoff runs and two victorious postseasons, and how I still get to brag that I was in attendance for Devon White's glorious catch in Game Three of the 1992 World Series. During my angst-ridden teen years and unfocused early twenties, my commitment to the game wasn't always consistent, but I continued to enjoy the quality time spent with my dad in the stands, away from all the distractions in our lives. A nuclear physicist by training, he devoted his busy work life to science and was governed primarily by logic. I was the more emotional one, fascinated by narrative and in love with the written word. Baseball was a perfect combination of our disparate passions and interests—chock-full of romantic feeling and myriad storylines, yet reliant on the measurements of complex statistics and the velocity of a ball travelling through space.

The game became a simple and necessary point of connection between us—a place where our interests aligned and we could communicate easily. While we didn't always agree, we could at least agree on baseball, if only on the fact that it was a really good way to spend an afternoon.

The experience of watching a live game with him also provided a rare window into who he was beyond just "my dad." A man of reason, he was always so cool and collected outside the ballpark that when he had a minor sports-related outburst in the bleachers, it reminded me that he had the capacity to care about things and, in turn, that he cared about me. His heckling of a bad call or his rejoicing over a home run was a reassuring thrill during my teenage years, when I was convinced he didn't understand me.

After I left home for good in the late nineties, the stadium became a place for us to reunite a few times a year and keep each other apprised of whatever was happening in our lives. "I'll meet you in your seat" was a common refrain. I usually arrived first, and then we'd sit side by side through nine innings, just like we'd always done. Around the fifth inning, one of us would ask "want to go for a wander?" when there was a lull in the on-field action, and we'd do a complete loop of the concourse together. On that walk, we'd buy a couple of hotdogs and some beers, check the score and the replays when necessary, and share stories from the months we'd been apart. He'd tell me about how his weekly darts league was doing, update me on our family back in England or on the vacations he and my mother were eagerly planning. I'd tell him about the literature and art classes I was taking at university, how my writing "career" was going, and the details of whatever demoralizing dead-end job I happened to have at the time.

The game ultimately kept us in touch, no matter how far away I'd roam, or how infrequent the phone calls became. A visit to the park gave us the time to just be a father and a daughter again, regardless of how selfishly caught up I was in the complicated minutiae of my own life. It also facilitated important and sometimes difficult conversations in a way nothing else did: the stadium was where I told my dad that I was thinking about getting married, and later, much to his barely concealed excitement, that my husband and I were thinking about starting a family. It's also where I finally confessed that we were having trouble conceiving, and that I needed his support. And there, among the cheering roar of baseball fandom, he gave me the parental hug I needed in the face of hardship. For us, things have always been easier at the ballpark, even when life dishes out its worst.

Maybe it's not surprising that my dad taught me a great deal of what I know about the game, but what is more important is that he did so in a way that always made me hungry to learn more. Never condescending or patronizing, he generously imparted his own growing understanding of all the plays and endless drama. He taught me about the ground rule double, the infield fly rule, and how the umpires' complicated schedules work. He never once pressured me to love baseball; instead, he gave me the knowledge and the space to discover my own unique brand of fascination. In fact, I credit him with not only helping me find a place for myself in baseball culture, but with fostering my own impulse to lay down the welcome mat for anyone who shows an interest in the game.

It was also my father who first instilled in me my now signature lack of worry when my team isn't on top—his love of the ballpark experience, combined with his patient, near-ambivalent view of the outcome, was always soothing, even when I didn't entirely understand the complexity of the rules or the stakes of any given matchup. "It was a good game," he'd always say on the way out of the stadium, whether it had been or not. For him—and then for us—baseball wasn't about competition, standings, or even winning. It was about being at the ballpark together, despite the sometimes less-than-perfect details. All that mattered to him was that we were there, an inheritance I'm grateful for.

At its core, baseball is a reliable community ritual in a constantly changing, secular world with fewer opportunities for real human connection. As we feel more and more isolated, and move further away from our families both physically and mentally, many of us are increasingly looking to spaces like ballparks to bring us together. So many baseball devotees I know have shared beautiful stories with me about the relationship between their fathers (or any kind of parental figure, really) and the ballpark. Those with more distant dads talk about the time spent there as special and sacred, the game bridging divides and providing a common love that is otherwise hard to find. Those who have lost their fathers remember days in the sun with a mixture of nostalgia and grief, their memories treasured more and more as time goes by. New dads speak enthusiastically about introducing their kids to the game they love—they buy tiny jerseys and ball caps, and strap their babies to their chests as they stroll the concourse, hoping their kids will find the same passion for it that they did.

So what exactly do you give the man who gave you the gift of baseball? More baseball it would seem. Last June, when the Jays decimated the Phillies at home, 11–3, via some hot bats and a Josh Donaldson grand slam, my dad and I did an early version of our annual Father's Day at the ballpark. I'm old enough now that I can buy the tickets and the beers myself, and the fact that he's retired means a noonday "businessman's special" game is a nice, relaxing way to spend an idle afternoon. As we usually do, we reminisced about games past, about heckling Oakland A's pitchers from above the bullpen in the 1992 ALCS, and of course about Devon White's legendary catch. We shared stories, worries, jokes, and three or so hours of the quality time that baseball always delivers.

I know that when it comes to fathers and baseball, I really lucked out. Even if the exclusionary world of sports didn't always make me feel welcome, my dad assured me that the ballpark was a place I deserved to be, and that I had a right to talk about this game. Our phone calls now often begin with him commenting on how my baseball team is doing, and when I get frustrated with the sports community and the abuse it can foster, he's there to remind me to keep pushing on.

Baseball is a game that many of us love to pass down to family members and friends; one that joins generations, and allows for long afternoons where seemingly disparate people can come together. A day at the park can act as a bonding exercise for many fathers, mothers, daughters, sons—whatever family you've chosen, or whatever family has chosen you.

And when it's at its very best, baseball can help us relate to one another—through victories, disappointments, and even a poorly belted out rendition of "Take Me Out to the Ball Game"—regardless of how different we can be.

WHAT BASEBALL STILL DOESN'T GET ABOUT INJURY AND MENTAL HEALTH

In 2009, while playing for the Baltimore Orioles, Ryan Freel was at second base when Boston Red Sox pitcher Justin Masterson hit him in the head with a pickoff throw. It wasn't the first time Freel had sustained a head injury on the field: two years earlier, he'd collided with his Cincinnati Reds teammate Norris Hopper, resulting in pain, headaches, and memory loss that prolonged his rehabilitation by weeks. By the time he retired in 2010, Freel, then thirty-four, had stated that he'd suffered nine or ten concussions over the course of his eight years in Major League Baseball.

Three years later, Freel was found dead in Jacksonville, Florida, from a self-inflicted shotgun wound.

His family, looking for answers, donated Freel's brain tissue to researchers studying chronic traumatic encephalopathy (CTE), a degenerative neurological condition that can only be diagnosed postmortem. The disease is typically found in people who have suffered multiple concussions and repeated head trauma (it was initially discovered in boxers), with symptoms including depression, apathy, anxiety, impaired cognition, and aggression. In December 2013, a year after Freel's death, the examination by the Center for the Study of Traumatic Encephalopathy revealed Freel had been suffering from Stage II CTE. He became the first MLB player to be diagnosed with the disease.

"It's a closure for the girls who loved their dad so much and they knew how much their dad loved them," Freel's mother told the media when the findings were released. "It could help them understand why he did what he did. Maybe not now, but one day they will."

The news brought some relief to the family, and it also helped initiate a desperately needed dialogue about the relationship between injury and mental health in what had previously been a culture of insidious silence. During his life, Freel seemed like a wild card: he'd been diagnosed with bipolar disorder, ADD (now known as ADHD), and depression, and was an alcoholic with anger and impulse-control issues. Now that we know the cause of his death, his story symbolizes the need to remove the stigma of mental illness in professional sports.

Though Freel's was the first official diagnosis in baseball, he joined a long, daunting list of professional athletes in other sports who have grappled with severe mental health issues as a result of injuries sustained in play. In the summer of 2013, the NFL reached a $765-million settlement with a group of more than 4,500 former players who alleged the league had not disclosed the dangers of concussion-related injuries to athletes. In November of that year, ten former NHL players filed a class action lawsuit claiming that the league had not done enough to protect them from brain trauma, and by February 2016 the number of complainants had jumped to 105. Instances of current and retired players seeking compensation are only becoming more frequent, with new lawsuits being launched, and more and more names added to existing claims.

In the book *League of Denial*, Mark Fainaru-Wada and Steve Fainaru's sweeping indictment of the NFL's health and safety policies, the list of players who have engaged in erratic, violent behaviour or suffered from confusion, depression, anxiety, and suicidal thoughts is staggering. The authors share stories of players losing their fortunes, shutting out or abusing their families, and ending their lives in a number of disturbing ways—from overdosing on painkillers, to shooting themselves in the chest, to drinking antifreeze.

For obvious reasons, major sports leagues do their best to play incidents such as these off as isolated events, yet when presented in a concentrated fashion, Fainaru-Wada and Fainaru's point becomes hard to ignore: mental health deterioration is epidemic, and fans, by way of their wilful blindness in the pursuit of personal enjoyment, are complicit.

Throwing-related injuries are the main cause of injury in Major League Baseball, but players with concussions ended up on the disabled list eighteen times in 2013, the year in which Freel's CTE was discovered postmortem. In an unexpected but welcome move, due in large part to head injuries, in 2014 Major League Baseball decided to prohibit "egregious" home-plate collisions. The rule change, as was probably to be expected, received mixed reactions from players past and present.

"The hitters wear more armor than the Humvees in Afghanistan," former major-league player and manager Pete Rose dismissively told the Associated Press. "Now you're not allowed to be safe at home plate? What's the game coming to? Evidently the guys making all these rules never played the game of baseball."

Former Blue Jays third baseman Brett Lawrie shared on social media: "I understand it's for the safety of the game but there's some things that I think should be left alone." Similarly, former catcher and current Detroit Tigers manager Brad Ausmus was quoted by CBS Sports as saying that although he agreed it was likely the "prudent" thing to do, he remained reluctant: "I am a little bit old school in the sense that I don't want to turn home plate into just another tag play. This is a run. This is the difference between possibly making the playoffs and not making the playoffs. It should matter a little bit more."

This is the status quo talking: when we're content to be "old school," it's easy to shrug off violence against players' bodies as integral to the game, even if it ultimately destroys their minds. There was a similar outcry when Major League Baseball implemented a new slide rule in 2016—a response to Chase Utley actually breaking Rubén Tejada's leg while coming in to a base. It would seem that, regardless of the outcome, the play always matters more than the player. So is it any wonder, then, that it's seemingly so difficult—and so controversial—for the culture of Major League Baseball to prioritize its players' health and well-being over the game?

"There's an expectation [from] the fanbase that says, 'I don't want to hear that you feel sad, because you make millions,'" Dirk Hayhurst said to me on the subject. Hayhurst is a former major-league pitcher and the author of *Bigger Than the Game*, a memoir that not only documents his struggles with injury, addiction, and mental illness, but also the punishment he felt he received for daring to speak candidly from the interior of baseball life. In 2014 I talked with him about this deep reluctance—from the leagues, the fans, and the athletes themselves—to discuss the mental health of active players.

"The perception is that, if you are very successful at a prestige job that we [associate with] fame, we perceive you as better and stronger than us," Hayhurst continued. "Even though we'll say we're all equal, we still perceive famous people as better and superior, and better and superior people who have been compensated should never feel sad. They should be totally inoculated against any of life's hardships. If we accept that [players] feel bad, we accept that a lot of things we hold dear are hollow."

Hayhurst's was among the voices that did speak out against plate collisions. "Take off the 'baseball players are commodities' glasses for a second and understand that they are people," he wrote in a piece for Sportsnet. "They're well compensated for playing a game that makes us think irrationally about how they should behave, but they're people all the same who will have [a] life after baseball."

This assertion that players are people, vulnerable like anyone else, is a tough one for sports culture to accept. Yet mental health is as much a part of an athlete's ability to perform as any other aspect of their well-being. And while the leagues are making clearer attempts to protect players from injuries that have a direct link to the function of their minds—MLB's approval of pitchers' padded protective caps; NFL rules preventing crown-of-the-helmet hits; the NHL outlawing avoidable checks to the head—they continue to fall short when it comes to addressing the more nuanced relationships between performance, injury, and mental health.

"[Some players] get so popular they have a legacy to

protect, or an image. It's like this gilded front," said Hayhurst. "They're 'so-and-so the product' or 'so-and-so the superhero in uniform,' and they're always thought of that way. There's a double-edged-sword effect. On one side, these guys are bigger than normal humans, [so] they're thought of as above and beyond. But on the other, in order to keep up that façade, you can't express broken things that make you look human."

In *Bigger Than the Game*, Hayhurst documents a shoulder injury that put him out of commission for the 2010 season, his subsequent descent into an abyss of crippling anxiety, his abuse of painkillers and sleeping pills, and a perceived lack of support from teammates and management. He told me he felt his injury had led them to desert him. "You would be amazed at how fast these guys . . . suddenly don't give a fuck about you because you're not healthy enough to help them win," he said. "You're dead. I thought we were family, we were brothers, and now all of a sudden I'm banished to some hole-in-the-wall training room. I don't hear from anybody. I might as well be dead."

Saddled with loneliness, self-loathing, violent mood swings, and "emotional freak-outs," Hayhurst's account underscores a distinct variation on the common connection between injury and the athlete's mental state—one that is rarely discussed. "You've internalized and made your identity out of [sports], and then injury just says you're gone," he said. "You may never come back to this. Everything will change. It doesn't only strip it away, it also isolates you in the process. And then you sit there on a training table, and you're like, there's no one patting me on the butt, there are no fans cheering for me, I have no value, I can't help my team." In the sad reality he describes in his book, athletes punish their bodies because it is asked of them—they are literally paid to do so—and they are then neglected or disposed of when the consequences of that punishment make it impossible for them to continue.

"This book talks about addiction," Hayhurst told me. "The strongest addiction any athlete will ever face is their addiction to [the] identity and adulation they get from being physically fit and doing their job."

At the time of our conversation, Hayhurst (who played for the San Diego Padres in 2008 and the Jays in 2009) painted a grim picture of a poisonous culture that denies and avoids the issue. Organizational efforts to assist players with mental health maintenance seem Kafkaesque in his depiction: the first time a player has "the mental health conversation" with a professional, he'll be in uniform, cleats on, glove in one hand, and a Gatorade or dip cup in the other. He'll be sitting outside on the grass, or maybe in the locker room, and a doctor will frame the conversation by telling him that, by following his advice, he'll perform better on the field. "He has to talk this way because he'll get tuned out by the players if he doesn't, and he'll also get fired by the organization," Hayhurst suggested. "The organization doesn't genuinely care about your mental health, unless . . . they spend a lot of money on you. They care about performance on-field. Everything in this realm has to be tweaked so it comes back to that one thing that baseball can quantify, which is production."

A poor or misguided level of care isn't the only issue; compounding it is a fundamental misunderstanding of what help is necessary in particular situations, and the cultural barriers to seeking it. "If injury isn't death, it's certainly a near-death experience," said Hayhurst. "It is a total life-changer. Athletes always say injury is the hardest thing, don't ever get injured. And I thought, yeah, it probably sucks—it's painful, surgery, a lot of question marks—but I had no idea [about] the psychological duress."

And even if the appropriate level of care were available, the clubhouse climate can make seeking help nearly impossible. "You can talk to your teammates about a lot of things," Hayhurst writes in *Bigger Than the Game*. "That you're angry, that you want to get drunk until you can't see straight, that you need them to keep a secret about cheating on your girlfriend. But you just don't talk about your emotions . . . Baseball players don't do that."

In fact, according to the book, players tend to steer clear of the team psychologist as if he were a threatening presence—someone who hangs around to weed out those not mentally strong enough for the sport. "Most of the players avoided him, especially in public," Hayhurst writes. "They called him a brain fuck, a blanket for the mentally weak, or a wet nurse for guys who can't handle the stress of baseball life. They'd beat their chests and say, 'If you can't handle the grind of the game, you don't belong in it.'" When I raised this passage with Hayhurst, he elaborated: "There are some resources. The problem is, if I turn to a mental resource, there's a stigma to me needing mental help, and that gets reported back to the organization." And a player runs the risk of such a report following him throughout his entire career.

This environment makes pursuing treatment for mental health issues difficult, according to Hayhurst, but it also discourages players from—and punishes them for—speaking out about said environment. In Jason Turbow's 2010 book *The Baseball Codes*, outspoken pitcher-turned-psychologist Tom House backs up this idea. "There are many things baseball manages to keep quiet about," he writes. "In fact, players who are foolish enough to discuss what went on in a closed clubhouse meeting . . . often turn up on other teams the next year." Add to this a lack of appropriate leadership—managers and coaches are not necessarily trained in successful management techniques; often, the main qualification is that you played the game, and ideally were good at it—and genuine, transparent conversations about how players are feeling become increasingly unlikely, if not impossible.

"If you are a headcase—and there have been a lot of headcases in this sport—but . . . a really successful headcase, it becomes part of your character. Everyone's okay with it," said Hayhurst. "If you're a fringe character, a fringe talent, you don't get that right. You get branded as weak or not able to hack it, or too much of an issue to worry about. So a lot of guys, instead of getting help, they choose to stay quiet." He told me some players choose to cope in more accepted fashions—namely, prescription drug use and abuse. Pills and booze become a popular way to self-medicate and avoid the stigma that comes with seeking real help. The upshot is a vicious cycle: a lack of professional support for those suffering from mental illness, and no safe way to speak out about it.

Since the release of Hayhurst's book in 2014, a handful of teams have tried more actively to address some of the mental health issues he described. In April 2015, the Associated Press reported that the Chicago Cubs, the Boston Red Sox, and the Washington Nationals were expanding their mental health support services. (The Cubs, for example, implemented a mental-skills program, while the Red Sox introduced one around behavioural health). As the AP notes, "While individual players have sought help with the mental side of the game for years, teams are responding to the changing attitudes [toward mental health issues] by offering more assistance to their players in this area."

More comprehensive programs are certainly an admirable, positive step forward, increasing support beyond that lone team psychologist who, according to Hayhurst, players have learned to avoid. But when it comes to mental health strategies, it can often feel like the league's focus is more about how said challenges affect a player's performance on the field—their "mental game"—than it is about an overarching concern for their well-being.

During a 2014 spring training game, Cincinnati Reds closer Aroldis Chapman was hit in the face by a line drive off the bat of Kansas City catcher Salvador Pérez. The initial pitch was clocked at 99 mph, and the sound the ball made colliding with Chapman's face was audible throughout the park. The stadium fell silent as he lay face down on the ground for several minutes, officials surrounding him, his legs twitching and cleats digging into the dirt of the pitcher's mound, in what appeared to be excruciating pain. The entire scene was a jarring reminder of the fallibility of the spectacle, and the vulnerability of its players.

Many of us who love sports understand we're making an uncomfortable choice to ignore certain aspects of its culture in order to enjoy ourselves. Racism, homophobia, sexism, DUIs, domestic abuse, physical violence, sexual assault, gambling, drugs—it can be a toxic culture, cloaked in large part by our fandom. This isn't lost on Hayhurst: "Everything is basically justified by how well you play on the field. If you're fantastic on the ball field, you can be a guy who beats your wife, has rage issues, has used performance-enhancing drugs. It has always been the case that performance covers over a multitude of sins. Baseball is full of horrible examples, but [some players] were good enough at the right time in their careers for us to forget how horrible they were."

It has been three years since I spoke to Dirk Hayhurst about his experience dealing with mental illness while playing major-league baseball, but he remains one of the few players who have talked publicly about these issues. While others have spoken openly about the stresses they have faced while playing the game—notably R.A. Dickey on his experience with trauma, Madison Bumgarner on wanting to go home while in the minors, and Adrian Cárdenas on the mental struggles that caused him to walk away from the game for good—it would seem that speaking out from the inside continues to be an unpopular move, and one with a great deal of stigma attached. Players risk being unfairly judged and disparaged, or having their concerns outright dismissed, not just by teammates and management, but also by fans—the "old school" ones; the ones who have bought into a mythical notion of toughness and "respecting the game"; the ones who would rather not see things change, even if that means turning a blind eye to what happens to players once they leave the field for the day.

Hayhurst may have betrayed a long-standing code by speaking out about his personal experiences, but his book reveals the danger of concealing them, and his decision to use his experience as a launching point is an admirable one. "I had to write [the book]," he told me, "because I had to figure out how to go on with the rest of my life. I needed this therapy. And I felt like if I needed it, other people probably needed it too."

A few days after taking that line drive to the face, Chapman posted a disturbing photo to his Instagram account: him in his hospital bed, with a crown of dozens of staples keeping his head closed post-surgery. Optimistic media reports relayed that Chapman suffered only a mild concussion and would return to throwing in a few weeks. Yet looking at that picture now, it's hard not to wonder if Chapman's injury may relate to a later incident, in October 2015, when he fired a gun eight times in his garage, and his girlfriend alleged he choked and pushed her against a wall. No charges were filed, but the player was later suspended thirty games under Major League Baseball's newly implemented domestic violence policy. (Chapman apologized for the "use of the gun" but denied hurting his girlfriend.) Though it's of course unwise to make casual connections or excuses for Chapman's behaviour, it is valuable to examine whether things could be different if Major League Baseball made prevention, recovery, and mental health support a priority.

We can't say conclusively, of course, whether Freel's life could have been saved or any other professional athlete's behaviour changed if they'd felt more comfortable seeking help for injury-related mental deterioration. Therapy doesn't deal in those sorts of absolutes. But as more players go through experiences like Freel's, it seems near-criminal not to at least start the conversation. If we invest in the game as fans, we likewise have a responsibility to invest in the long-term health and safety of its players. We're well past the point where wilful blindness can be considered any sort of excuse.

THE RUNNER ON THIRD

"Ultimately the thing that helped me find some healing [was when] I learned that life was not about turning the page, or getting to the other side of something. It's about holding what is broken about the world and holding what is joyful about the world, and being able to take a step forward with both. That is living well in the moment. And that's what I've tried to make a discipline of."

R.A. DICKEY

A few years back, I got a baseball tattoo.

You could say it was an ill-advised and impulsive decision, and you'd certainly be right: the decision to get permanently inked was indeed a spontaneous one, but in my defence, I will say it was the culmination of a great deal of thought.

It was 2013 when I decided to walk into my local tattoo shop, a year when the Jays went 74–88, came dead last in the AL East, and were a demoralizing twenty-three games back in their division. I had just come out of a long stint of labour-intensive counselling following a long overdue PTSD diagnosis, which meant spending countless hours on a therapist's little grey couch, and countless evenings and afternoons watching my boys in blue win—and mostly lose—baseball games. Though I was still exhausted from the hard work inherent to that therapeutic journey, I felt like I was pretty much out of the woods. (The woods being the place where I didn't feel like a fully functional human being who could feed herself properly or sleep with any regularity.)

Because baseball had kindly accompanied me on that exhausting trip through my own trauma, I suppose I wanted to thank it with some sort of permanent homage. So, in the company of a couple of close, supportive friends, I went under the needle and got three simplified, stylized bases inked on the inside of my right wrist, the third coloured in solid black. If you follow baseball closely enough, you'll know that this tiny inch-or-so-wide image means there's a runner on third. It means there's still potential and possibility. It means you are, at least in the context of my right arm, always in scoring position. It means you're just ninety feet away from change (actually more like eighty-eight, but that's not really the point). It means you can come back, and that hope isn't totally lost.

It was a fitting metaphor at the time, just as it is a fitting metaphor now.

As a person who has dealt with terrible anxiety throughout my life, I'm comfortable admitting that I find myself in near-constant need of the (now physical) reminder that things will be okay, and that even if they're not okay, there's a high likelihood I'll be fine regardless. Even the best and most thoughtful humans I know tend to have short memories when it comes to their own ability to conquer the struggles they face. They fail to give themselves credit for what they've overcome, and forget to tell themselves that if they got through that last terrible thing, there's a good chance that they'll get through this one as well. Since I started viewing this game as a metaphor for how to live a better life, I see this phenomenon both on the field and in my day-to-day. I see it in the general feelings of fans, and in my own sense of loss, distress, and dire disappointment, baseball-related and otherwise.

At some point in my life, I decided that baseball was the one place where I would try to be optimistic despite myself. I've never been much for self-helpy or shallow inspirational statements, or the idea that if you "purge the bad feelings from your life," all of a sudden things will be better, but I need to believe in this one thing. I need to remember pitcher R.A. Dickey's clubhouse-locker notecard that says "no negativity allowed" and apply that sentiment liberally to my own life. Frankly, there are far too many places where we feel hopeless and traumatized by what the world dishes out, and here, in the world of baseball, I choose admiration, love, respect, and delirious hope above all things. I choose to be inspired by the men who play this game, and how much they love each other while doing so. And though it is perhaps naive, unprofessional, and maybe even stupid (and an easy subject of mockery), I choose optimism in baseball because it is the better, healthier choice for both pre- and post-tattoo me.

Whenever I desperately worry about on-field outcomes, I look at that self-dictated marking on my wrist and remind myself that my worry is a luxury. If my primary life-anxieties are presently built around something as frivolous as whether or not the Blue Jays will beat the Red Sox tonight, I should be pretty damn grateful for the gift of that worry. A blown save, for example, is not the stuff of disease, depression, loss, or grief. It's just bats, and balls, and men doing their very best.

I am convinced that watching sports makes us better people. What other arena offers both an escape from the trials of life and a place to diligently learn how to live it, a place to both relax and do the necessary work of becoming more human? I certainly know this game has helped me become whole in ways I didn't think possible, made me care about and connect to things outside myself when

I was feeling isolated and insular, made me take things as they come rather than agonize about every possible future outcome. Nine innings has given me a place to accept the most hated aspects of myself, and helped me not to feel so bad about them after all.

Baseball has taught me that it is possible to be totally consumed by worry, and at the same time not to worry at all. It has taught me to let go and accept what plays out in front of me, understanding that no matter how much I need a win, I will never have any control over what happens. For an anxious person like myself, that's an incredible lesson, one that I chose to learn through dozens of nail-biting, fist-clenching matchups. Baseball has also taught me that a win can be someone else's loss, and that people can always surprise you in ways both good and bad. Less-than-reliable Josh Thole can hit a much-needed RBI or two, and ultimate underdog Chris Colabello can be suspended for a positive PED test. A once-derided J.A. Happ can end up in the Cy Young conversation, and a generally steadfast Marco Estrada can give up some unexpected home runs. The last-place team can demoralize the first-place team. The hero is sometimes totally predictable, and sometimes it's who you'd least expect. And sometimes your boys in blue can come from behind and score twelve runs, eight of which are in a single inning.

This game has consistently asked me to have high expectations, and at the same time asked me not to have any at all. It has demanded I be fluid, and open, and generous, and in the moment. To readily accept the possibility of defeat, yet dream endlessly of victory. To live a life of faith, hope, and endless enthusiasm, and to know that anything is possible. It has asked me to always see meaning in the meaningless, and asked me to close my eyes tight and make a wish or two, regardless of the knowledge that it won't have any effect on the outcome.

More than anything else, baseball has taught me, time and again, that we can and we do get better.

Sportswriter and friend Jessica Kleinschmidt once said, during the thick of anxious September baseball, "I think we are looking for someone who loves us even when we aren't winning." To be honest, I'm not sure if she was referring to life or to the game, but then I'm also not sure it matters. Those people who really matter to me are the ones who loved me during that terrible time before the tattoo, when I always felt like I was losing, when I was hopeless and useless and probably not very fun to be around. The friends I value are the ones who are willing to let me be genuine about my failures and my fears, who care about me even when I'm less than victorious, when I'm shitty, and tired, and bad at life. When I'm swinging and swinging and swinging and never really seem to connect. When I'm giving up home runs no matter how hard I try to do otherwise. When the ball just keeps sailing over my head.

I know I am lucky to be passionate about baseball. I acknowledge that it matters to me because I have the room in my life for it to matter. But after what I have been through, I am thankful for the space to love and to care for something more than I would have ever thought possible.

When the September-baseball grind sets in, part of me always misses the "it's early" part of the season, when a game is just a full-of-possibility sunny pleasure, and not a terrifying roller-coaster ride of unhinged emotion. But in times of uncertainty and disappointment, when things seem dire and nothing seems to get better, it always helps to be reminded that there's a metaphoric runner on third. We're in scoring position. We can always come back.

And hell, even if we don't, we'll be okay.

JOSÉ FERNÁNDEZ, 1992–2016

◆◇◇

> "I like to have fun. I want for people to say he was always having fun. I want people to say he was a hard worker, that he's not going to give up. That's it. That's all I can ask."
>
> JOSÉ FERNÁNDEZ

I often describe the reason I write as a deep desire to make people (including myself) feel a little better about the pain and confusion they endure. Fundamentally, I want to bring solace and companionship to those who are feeling alone. Yet there are moments in a writing life when you realize just how futile the act really is, and that no matter how hard you try, the words will never salve the monumental emotions at hand.

Grief, more than any other human emotion, seems to violently reject any offered comfort, written or otherwise. Even when we grieve for those we loved but didn't know directly, the emotion is near impossible to temper. Grief makes us question things like justice and order, tests our belief in fairness and our trust in the comfort and stability we rely on. Grief is beyond our control, is its own rabid animal, asking only that we surrender to it, while it refuses to be calmed or contained. One must wait out its painful stay until it finally decides to leave—and anyone who has experienced grief knows that, though its presence lessens over time, it never really leaves.

Despite the fact that words can never salve the feelings inherent to the loss of a beloved human being, grief certainly comes with its own stock phrases. When someone dies, there are handfuls of helpless little words we string together that, by virtue of their own futility, only emphasize how impossible consolation can really be. *Terrible tragedy. Thoughts and prayers. A great loss.* We throw these sentiments out into the world knowing that there is really nothing that can be said or written, no gesture or tribute made, that can ever make it okay. For those who are mourning, nothing will ever be okay, and in a world where we constantly look for solutions, that is deeply debilitating.

On the morning of September 25, 2016, twenty-four-year-old Marlins pitcher José Fernández was killed in a Miami boating accident, marking the end to the short life of someone who had overcome and offered so much. At the age of fifteen, after being jailed for a previous attempt to defect, Fernández successfully left Cuba on his fourth try. He was a teenage boy who selflessly saved his mother from drowning in the turbulent waters on their way to the U.S. via Mexico. "I dove [into the water] to help a person, not thinking who that person was. Imagine when I realized it was my own mother. If that does not leave a mark on you for the rest of your life, I don't know what will." In 2013, he was finally reunited with the grandmother he had been forced to leave behind, fulfilling his dream of having her see him pitch at the major-league level. "Everything I do is for her," he said, just before he was tearfully surprised by her appearance at Marlins Park.

When he died, Fernández had only recently announced that he and his girlfriend were expecting a child, and while the loss of anyone, especially someone so young, is devastating, this detail is one that haunts many. Further, Fernández was genuinely admired and celebrated by all those who knew him. He was a player who, while incredibly gifted in his role as a Marlins pitcher, transcended team allegiances to become a symbol of the absolute elation this game brings to so many. By all accounts, he was the human distillation of unabashed enthusiasm. Few players were so transparent about their genuine passion, or so open with their exuberance and childlike glee when magic happened on the field. Marlins manager Don Mattingly said that Fernández "played with the joy of a Little Leaguer," and it was because of that joy that he allowed so many to experience irrepressible, unfettered, and unfiltered happiness through him.

It is true that we sometimes turn to baseball to find an escape from our personal pain, so when pain appears in the game in such dramatic fashion it can be desperately hard to work through. Yes, we often don't know these men who bring us so much unending comfort, but we genuinely love them regardless, allowing them into our hearts and lives in ways that constantly surprise us. For a time, we live by their narratives, both on the field and off, and feel so many necessary emotions through their very public successes and struggles.

What is truly awful about this tragedy is not only the loss of a person who was beautiful, and kindhearted, and full of a limitless, infectious happiness, but how it devastated so many who called him a teammate, colleague, or friend. Seeing men like the Boston Red Sox's David Ortiz, the L.A. Dodgers' Yasiel Puig, and the entire Marlins roster grieve was, quite simply, heartbreaking, and a reminder that underneath the competition and rivalry of Major League Baseball there are myriad friendly affinities and deep connections that mean so much more than the game itself. In fact, this terrible loss somehow rendered baseball both entirely meaningful and entirely meaningless, asserting that for all our anxiety over wins and losses, the thing that matters most is how this game brings out our shared humanity. It is a lesson we are all in need of, and one that was taught in the most cruel and unfair way.

Baseball deals a lot in what is "meaningful" and what is not, and that meaning always seems to be attributed to whether there's some great Gatorade-showered glory at stake. We say that some games matter and others don't, and our blood pressure levels are dictated accordingly. But the truth is, come winter, I know that I would do anything for just one more so-called meaningless game, because it would, as always, help me through so very much. Every single damn game, all season long, matters so much because baseball consistently gives us not only a place to escape from all the hardships in our lives, but the very tools we need to heal from them.

After news broke of Fernández's death, his number 16 was stencilled on the back of the pitcher's mound at Marlins Park. When the team eventually returned to their field after a cancelled game against the Braves, every member wore that same number on their jerseys, and somehow managed to play through their grief. Leading off the bottom of the first inning, Marlins second baseman Dee Gordon hit a home run off the first pitch he faced, weeping openly as he ran the bases before making a gesture to the heavens and falling into his teammates' arms. It was the only home run Gordon had hit all season long, one that the left-handed hitter batted right while wearing his fallen teammate's helmet in tribute.

"I ain't never hit a ball that far, even in [batting practice]," said Gordon postgame. "I told the boys, 'If you all don't believe in God, you better start.' For that to happen today, we had some help."

There is no real roadmap for dealing with the kind of inexplicable grief that comes with the death of someone we didn't know. Though the loss is not personal by definition, it leaves a hole in a community and a culture. While we can understand that our suffering will never be as great as that of those who were close to Fernández, we still feel its vicious sting. And though it is true that nothing can be said or written that will assuage that kind of acute, relentless sadness, it is certainly okay to talk about it. It is okay to acknowledge the terrible feelings, to mourn a missing and vital piece of something we hold so close, and to feel immense empathy for the men who suffer this sudden wound and then unbelievably go back to the diamond to play on.

I hate that it often takes a terrible, tragic event for us to gain necessary perspective. I hate that we had to lose the passionate, joyful gift that was pitcher José Fernández to be reminded that so much of what we worry about in a baseball season is entirely irrelevant in the grander scheme—a truth I think we always know deep down anyway. As the Marlins gathered around the mound after beating the Mets, 7–3, arms slung around each other's shoulders before they stepped forward and placed their caps down in reverence, I realized that there would be no single game more important than that one all season long, and no other home run as important as Dee Gordon's.

Hearing the Miami crowd chant José's name, as his teammates kneeled and wept in the red infield dirt, I was reminded exactly why this game is so very important to so many. Though all these words feel particularly empty right now, they deserve to be said: we shouldn't take the comfort and gifts of baseball, the value of life, or each other for granted.

"You fucking show up, man, and you fucking play the game hard and that's it—that's my line. That's it. There's no fucking secret. You play the game. Period. There's no magic way of doing things, you just keep doing what you've been doing the whole way."

RUSSELL MARTIN

in response to the Blue Jays being down two games to Cleveland in the 2016 ALCS

"It's that fine line of not being stubborn but also not chasing your tail either. You've just got to trust in what you're doing. When I go out and I execute and I do what I'm supposed to do, it's going to work out. That has to be the mindset. As a bullpen guy, this game can be a roller coaster ride. I know it's a cliché, but all those clichés are there for a reason."

DREW STOREN

"Hey buddy, want to go to a playoff game?"

TROY TULOWITZKI

on the phone with his two-year-old son, Taz, during the Jays' 2016 postseason celebration

BASEBALL ANXIETY IS GOOD FOR YOU

I have a baseball confession to make. I have spent a lot of my time at postseason games hiding out in the women's washroom. When the score is close, and every pitch matters, I have a tendency to retreat quickly to the concourse, temporarily stepping away from the action in the hope that when I return to my seat, everything will have worked out okay.

I realize that hiding in a stall, or turning on the tap so I can't actually hear the sold-out crowd's reactions to what is happening on the field, is an odd and perhaps self-defeating habit for a rabid baseball fan to have. But as someone who has battled severe anxiety for most of my adult life, I've found it's the only way I can get through the trials and triumphs of October baseball.

In early 2008, I was diagnosed with generalized anxiety disorder. By the time I managed to get myself to a doctor, I was desperate for some sort of reprieve—my physical symptoms were so bad that I was experiencing multiple panic attacks a day, and as a result I was terrified to leave my house. Simple outings, the kind that the mentally well take for granted—parties, dinners, concerts, book launches—had become difficult for me and, as is often the case with anxiety sufferers, I started avoiding them altogether. Soon my intensifying agoraphobia and claustrophobia made it impossible for me to be out in public. I found it hard to ride in a car or take the subway, use an elevator or sit in a movie theatre. Even a short walk to the corner store to pick up a carton of milk felt daunting.

Anxiety tricks you into believing that everything is dire and that the worst is always about to happen. For me, the world became an overwhelming, threatening place I no longer wanted to be in. I was afraid of a laundry list of innocuous things. I felt unsafe when there was no reason to feel unsafe, and in an act of self-protection I eventually isolated myself and ended up a recluse. It was a vicious cycle, one that I could not break on my own, and so after that initial diagnosis in a fluorescent-lit doctor's office, and under the recommendation of a friend, I started seeing a cognitive behavioural therapist.

My therapist worked out of Toronto's Centre for Addiction and Mental Health, and her specialty was anxiety disorder and its many physical manifestations, making her the perfect person to help me with my sweaty, gasping panic, the pervasive lump in my throat, and the numbness in my extremities. When I first started seeing her, I had panic attacks in the cab on the way to her office building, and in the elevator up to her floor, and in the waiting room outside her office. The pattern on the carpet and the framed paintings of flowers in the lobby made me dizzy, and I would read photocopied pamphlets from the information rack to distract myself until she opened her door to usher me in.

Her goal-oriented brand of psychotherapy focused on my flawed emotional reactions and my irrational thoughts in the face of the unknown. She spoke to me about "free-floating anxiety," the idea that worry is an amorphous thing looking for something to cling to, even when there is—as was true in my case—really nothing to worry about. The goals that we mapped out in our one-hour sessions were as basic as my leaving the house again, taking short trips on the subway, and taking a long, luxurious shower without fear of my imminent demise. (Yes, I was actually afraid I would slip, fall, and die in the shower.) I had to be willing to expose myself to the things I was afraid of so that the fear would eventually dissipate.

Thanks to a rigorous and regimented plan of consistent exposure therapy, within eight weeks my life miraculously returned to something I could handle, all because I was willing to subject myself to the very things that stoked my anxiety. I got better precisely because I chose to face the things I feared the most.

Though I'm far from the person I was when anxiety disorder made me a shut-in, I still experience distress when watching baseball games that matter. It took me a very long time to realize this truth—for years, the matchups I watched with interest were largely inconsequential, because my team was usually hovering toward the bottom of the standings. Trips to the ballpark were merely an escapist exercise where wins and losses barely meant a thing. But when the 2015 season rolled around, and the Blue Jays looked to be legitimate postseason contenders, I had to face the fact that my anxiety was following me to the very place I had so often gone to avoid it.

Maybe it's because of my mental health struggles, or maybe it's the same for anyone who's devoted to a team in contention, but when a particular game is important, I spend a lot of time watching it from behind my hands. I turn the broadcast on and then off and then on again, or hide until a key inning is over. I'll often leave my stadium seat to pace nervously on the concourse, as if watching the game on a television next to the hot dog vendor will somehow shield me from any pain. When the season's on the line, I am usually filled with dread, and no matter what happens—no matter how big my team's lead is, no matter how much it seems we've got this one in the bag—it is impossible for me to get comfortable until that very last out. There is a reason why some of the most compelling shots during a playoff baseball game are those of struggling fans biting their nails and clutching their caps in all-consuming worry.

In a lot of ways, attending do-or-die baseball games feels like the exposure therapy I threw myself into in 2008. Whether consciously or not, for those hoping to learn how to better cope with the chaos life dishes out, a stressful matchup can be a sheltered training ground. After all, fans voluntarily subject themselves to baseball's multiple stressors while believing that everything will turn out just fine, and even if it doesn't, there's the understanding that it really is only a game. Objectively, it's a safe way to test our endurance without any of those pesky dire consequences. (I will be forever thankful that I managed to keep my scared self focused on the diamond when José Bautista hit his seventh-inning, home run during Game Five of the 2015 ALDS against the Texas Rangers.) And not only do so many of us fans crave and wholeheartedly immerse ourselves in the worst kind of sports anxiety, we actually pay for it with our ticket, jersey, and hot dog purchases. We're happy to participate in something we are deeply afraid will break our hearts, because we know, no matter the outcome, it makes our lives richer and better.

Nowhere is this more true than around the postseason, and the 2016 Toronto Blue Jays certainly offered advanced-level exposure therapy for the anxiety-stricken.

When the team's offence started to fall apart at the beginning of September, losing their once-secure AL East lead to the feisty and fierce Boston Red Sox, Toronto fans knew the rest of the month would be a terrifying battle to the bitter end. For the Jays, every single game counted, right up to that 2–1 win over the Red Sox on October 2. Winning the last game of the regular season dictated that the Jays would host the Orioles at home in a single do-or-die wild card game to decide who went on to the division series.

I wish I knew more about the actual science behind what happens to your mind and body after long periods of bouncing back and forth between extreme emotional peaks and valleys. I experienced so many dramatically different baseball feelings that September—I screamed and leapt with joy, and cried and fell into misery—that my body was broken and my long-praying soul was a foggy mess of overuse. I was so exhausted, both physically and mentally, that I could have slept for a few days straight, except sleep, sadly, became impossible—I invested myself in the outcome of every single game, and that investment came with a liberal dose of insomnia. There was no luxurious early clinch, where a handful of end-of-season games could be played without fear. The Blue Jays didn't even get the comfort of a five-game series to start their October playoff run.

All of that said, I willingly, and yes, happily, watched every moment. (Well, when I wasn't hiding in the washroom.) I surrendered to the love of something I just couldn't control, because my past experience had taught me that it was a good and healthy thing for me to do.

When I nervously put on my blue cap and T-shirt on the afternoon of the 2016 American League wild card game, I wasn't exactly confident that the Jays would be able to squeeze their way into the ALDS. That doesn't mean I wasn't hanging on to my signature baseball optimism, or a resolute belief in my team's tenacity. It just means I was uneasy during every moment of that matchup, peering at plays through my fingers, and I felt tormented through every at-bat. It means I prayed, and I wished, as if my personal conviction could somehow affect the result. In fact, when my dad very kindly called during the game to see how I was doing, I informed him that I was "busy concentrating."

José Bautista graced us with a solo homer in the second, and Michael Saunders went home on Ezequiel Carrera's single in the fifth, but after that action the teams were deadlocked for five more unbearable innings. The crowd lived and died by every pitch, white-knuckling it as steadfast closer Roberto Osuna managed to make it out of the ninth without giving up a run. Going into the tenth, it genuinely felt like the game would never end, that we would be stuck in our debilitating baseball misery forever.

And then, after all the fear, fervour, and frenzy that filled the Rogers Centre that unseasonably warm October evening, there was a quiet, tiny gasp of a moment. It happened at 11:33 p.m., in the bottom of the eleventh inning, with two men on and one out. After an audible crack when Edwin Encarnación connected with a pitch from Ubaldo Jiménez, and just before the ball sailed easily over the left-field wall, Encarnación stood there, taking it all in. He knew, the entire Jays dugout knew, and the 49,934 fans in the stands knew, that the Blue Jays' painful road to the postseason had in fact been well worth the slog. All that agony was what allowed us to feel the best baseball feelings possible. Hope. Relief. Elation. Joy. Gratitude.

In the replay of that incredible wild card game-winning, walk-off home run, there is a shot of a smiling woman in the stands, exuberantly clutching her homemade sign that reads "Never Say Die." It's a phrase that best characterizes everything we had endured as Blue Jays fans up until that glorious point, and perfectly captures a month of baseball that, on any given game day, felt painfully up in the air, if not hanging by a thread. And after all that waiting and all that worry, Encarnación threw his arms above his head and then dramatically tossed his bat away in glorious triumph. "It was pretty similar to [Bautista's] home run last year, to be honest," said Osuna of Encarnación's walk-off blast. "It was unbelievable."

Unbelievable is definitely a good word to use to describe what happened in those final moments. Yes, much like the previous year's now-mythic Game Five of the ALDS, the drama felt scripted, even clichéd, as if it were an inspirational film plot constructed solely for maximum impact. The whole affair was baseball at its most harrowing and emotionally manipulative, leaving everyone in the stadium blissfully exhausted and psychologically hungover in its wake. After dealing with the occasional temptation to question why I love this game so much, especially when it has such a capacity to disappoint and distress, I can thank Encarnación for generously giving me my answer.

I've long thought that one of the cruellest (yet necessary) things about the game of baseball is that it's always at its very best when the lead-up to victory is a terrible onslaught of uncertainty, and when the unbelievable has to fight its way to becoming believable. If at any point that win had felt safe, secure, and inevitable, the outcome would not have been as delicious. It's difficult not to think that fans are actually better off for how hard that game was, despite the fact that we may not have felt that way when it went into excruciating extra innings.

If I am a person characterized by my struggle with irrational anxiety, what does it mean that I so willingly subject myself to a tight pennant race and these vital do-or-die games? That I make myself vulnerable to something that brings me so much anguish? It turns out that uncertainty and anxiety—two feelings that have tormented me for much of my adult life—are the best ingredients for producing baseball magic, something you'll only experience if you're willing to expose yourself to them. It's an important reminder that true beauty and fulfillment can often only be found when we're willing to face our struggles head-on.

My personal experience of anxious, clinical rock bottom seems like a lifetime ago now, but the knuckle-biting matchups of 2016 certainly reminded me of those dark times—not because I felt compelled to have rolling panic attacks over a baseball game, but because now that I am "better," I can endure and even invite the tension, the cold sweats, and the nausea that kind of experience can bring. I expose myself to all of it for one simple reason—because I know the ultimate reward that comes with watching a ball fall on the other side of that outfield wall.

BIG BAD BAUTISTA

"I don't think I take pride in being a hated guy. Absolutely not. I don't think I'm a guy who does things purposely to get hated. If me helping my team win ball games and me having to go about it the way that I have to in order to be the best player I can be, make some people hate me, so be it. What can I do? Start some sort of nationwide tour to prove to people that I'm a nice guy? I'm sure there's more people that actually like me than the ones that don't. It's just that the ones that don't seem to be a little bit more loud."

JOSÉ BAUTISTA, OCTOBER 5, 2015

After a twenty-one-year drought, the Toronto Blue Jays going to the playoffs for two straight years in 2015 and 2016 afforded plenty of room to build narratives around the team. There were some beautiful, heart-warming high points, like the triumphant 2015 return of long-injured pitcher Marcus Stroman, with his proud, weeping father watching him from the stands. There were some embarrassing low points, like a bizarrely generated "conflict" that same year between pitchers R.A. Dickey and David Price (it didn't exist), and a distracting 2016 story about the team having a beef with certain members of the media. With lots of column inches to fill and a growing public hunger for stories, it became difficult to keep up with all the mini-dramas that were being documented and, at times, manufactured.

One of the most enduring subjects of the team's post-season triumphs was that of José Bautista's controversial personality. Both years, the baseball media at large did an excellent job perpetuating a Bautista-as-villain tale, and non-Jays fans lapped it up in the interest of justifying their desire for Toronto's elimination. Detractors seized upon and disseminated quotes from opposing players and managers that highlighted Bautista's arrogance, his vanity, and his "disrespect for the game." And while the entire city of Toronto rejoiced over Bautista's aggressively flipped bat in that explosive 2015 ALDS Game Five, a debate erupted around whether or not the right fielder's behaviour was appropriate.

"I told [Edwin Encarnación] José needs to calm that down, just kind of respect the game a little more," Texas Rangers pitcher Sam Dyson told the *Washington Post*. "He's a huge role model for the younger generation that's coming up playing this game, and I mean he's doing stuff that kids do in wiffle ball games and backyard baseball. It shouldn't be done." Another Rangers pitcher, Derek Holland, added his disdain to the chorus of "Bad Bautista," saying, "I mean, personally, I don't like him, either."

In the media, the number of pieces asking the question *Was the bat flip acceptable?* was astounding. Many ignored the cultural (and racist) implications of even having the discussion at all. Bat-flipping is common practice in the Dominican Republic, the birthplace of Bautista and eighty-three other players on Opening Day 2015, and yet it's regarded with disdain within the predominantly white North American baseball establishment. Further, because Toronto lacked an obvious evildoer, it became necessary to pick on Bautista's now legendary pride and self-love in the interest of engineering drama and demonizing the team: *He's full of himself; he "mouths off" to the media; he's "explosive" and "inappropriate"; he stares down opponents; he messes with misbehaving fans by denying them free baseballs; he thinks he's "better than the game."* Somehow Bautista morphed into a big bad bully on the playground, and according to many, he needed to be taken down a peg. (It's pretty clear what old-school baseball—and sports culture in general—means when it makes that suggestion to a man of colour.)

Bautista became a figure of such disdain that when Rangers second baseman Rougned Odor punched Bautista in the jaw during a Jays versus Rangers series in May 2016, Texas fans very openly celebrated Bautista "getting what was coming to him." By the time the Jays met up with Texas again in the 2016 ALCS, Rangers supporters had made clear their refusal to let anyone forget that Odor had landed that blow—there were handmade signs and T-shirts commemorating the punch, and even a lifetime offer of free BBQ for Rougned Odor. It seemed an attempt at widespread humiliation was now a valid form of retribution for all of Bautista's supposed arrogant talk and misbehaviour. (Bautista refused to be humiliated by Texas. With the Jays easily sweeping the series, and Bautista *gently* laying down his bat after a Game One three-run home run, we now know who really got the last laugh.)

Thing is, there's absolutely nothing wrong with the way José Bautista acts. If you strip away the baseball world's incessant buzz and convenient media sound bites, its whining about hallowed unwritten rules and "respecting the game," you'll actually realize that he's not only the sports hero Toronto desperately wants, he's the hero Major League Baseball desperately needs. I could make this argument by saying Bautista is a good, hard-working, successful guy, because there's certainly a huge amount of available evidence to support that idea. The six-time All-Star has over a decade of major-league experience at six different positions, is a three-time Silver Slugger, and has twice taken home the Hank Aaron Award as the American League's top hitter. He's also made a side project of advocating against performance-enhancing drugs, is a married father of three, and a successful, stylish business entrepreneur who founded the Bautista Family Education Fund, an organization that sponsors aspiring baseball players' postsecondary-education costs. On top of all that, during a 2016 rehab stint with the minor-league Buffalo Bisons, he bought all postgame meals for not only the entire team, but for the opposing teams as well.

While it's clear that Bautista is a talented player who does good work both on the field and off, I'd actually argue that it's the less "likeable" aspects of his behaviour that truly secure his hero status. He won't bow to incessant, ingrained expectations about the way athletes should speak or act in public, nor will he buy into any of the press's ridiculous quote-twisting assertions about who he really is. During a spring 2016 scrum, he refused to talk about that jubilant Game Five bat flip, noting that if he wanted his authentic feelings out in the world, he'd share them via his own channels: "What I say doesn't matter, because you're going to do with it what you want, so I don't want to waste my time elaborating," he told *USA Today* reporter Ted Berg. "If I would say it, I would say it in my own direct line to fans, so I know it's not going to get misconstrued . . . I've got a couple more followers, I believe, than you and maybe all the media in here combined, so I've got a bigger reach. More people are going to listen to what I say on my direct line anyway."

It's obvious Bautista doesn't suffer (media) fools and refuses to toe the MLB party line despite unsolicited advice to the contrary. (When he was with the Pirates, he even refused to wear his team-issued socks the way he was supposed to.) He's openly criticized sports personalities for their racism, as was the case with him calling out ESPN's Colin Cowherd for comments that implied players from the Dominican Republic aren't very smart. He's also responsible for one of the more hilarious responses in baseball Twitter history: when *Toronto Sun* sports columnist Steve Simmons baited Bautista with a tweet, the slugger responded, very simply, "who are you and why are you talking to me?"

During the summer of 2015, Bautista engaged in a three-month boycott of one-on-one Sportsnet interviews because he believed the network took advantage of rookie and friend Devon Travis by refusing to reimburse him for a suit he purchased during a segment. (No small gesture on Bautista's part, given Sportsnet is owned by Rogers Media, and Rogers owns the Blue Jays.) And on October 17, 2015, he took to Twitter to blast the media's suggestion that he had thrown teammate Ryan Goins under the bus regarding a missed pop fly: "I challenge ANYONE to play the full tape of my postgame interview and then make your own conclusions. Nice try."

Bautista's so-called diva-esque attitude of self-importance is talked about as being a bad example for kids watching and playing the game. I question why we want to teach young people—especially those who are marginalized—not to be openly proud of their accomplishments. In doing so, we suggest to them that praising their success is a flaw, and that believing in themselves is an embarrassing secret to be hidden away. Bautista's on-field presence, the way he conducts himself in media scrums, even the way he tweets (@JoeyBats19) all indicate a secure self-reliance that I'm happy to see inspire the wrongly insecure. He's chided for admiring his achievements, but really, why shouldn't he (and all of us) celebrate them? And if baseball's mired traditions are notorious for being violent, racist, sexist, and homophobic, why should he respect the game at all?

Reimagining this "disrespectful" and "arrogant" Bautista caricature as firmly on the side of good is an excellent exercise. He's confident and loyal, defends and supports his teammates, and patently refuses to let anyone speak for him. He won't put up with anyone's shit and doesn't believe anyone else should either. He asserts his humanity in a gossipy media landscape that seeks to rob him of it. And while his opponents and detractors are shrieking "what about the children!" he's actively inviting said children into the clubhouse to snap selfies with him, before riding home from the game on his team scooter.

When it comes right down to it, José Bautista *is* the Toronto Blue Jays. It's actually hard not to think of him as the very centre of the team—the unofficial captain, the spokesperson, the go-to image, and the brand itself. On a roster of immense talent, multiple stars, and one pretty-damn-charismatic MVP named Josh Donaldson, Bautista unquestionably remains the defining face of the organization. I would even go so far as to guess there are more Bautista jerseys out in the world than any other name on the team. He's the easy favourite player, the T-shirt you put on your toddler, the guy whose opinion you really want to know, and the only sound bite you need.

"I wear my emotions on my sleeve," Bautista once said when asked about that scandalous (but totally justified) bat flip. "I think that's what gives me my drive—that's what keeps me going and allows me to be successful. I have to play like that—if I don't, then I might not be me."

Though other teams may have hated him enough to punch him in the face, having someone like that as one of your own is a defiant and defining badge of honour—a living, breathing "fuck you" to anyone who decides to be judgmental, critical, or hateful. When he was activated from that month-long stint on the disabled list during the 2016 season, you could almost hear a collective, citywide sigh of relief. It hardly mattered that he debuted with just a walk and a single. We were simply grateful he was there at the plate with his fierce, mouthguarded face.

Most of us simply aren't proud or arrogant enough about our own successes. We don't stick up for ourselves—or for the things and the people we care about—out of fear. We could benefit from following Bautista's blazing lead. Our heroes don't always have to be nice to everyone, especially not to those who deliberately humiliate, misinterpret, or insult them, nor do they need to fall in line with a system that seeks to muzzle them. José Bautista knows he's good because he is. He isn't afraid to be authentic, and won't let anyone tell him to shut up, sit down, and take it. And we love him for it.

I can't imagine a better message being delivered to young fans—nor a better kind of baseball hero for them to look up to.

"Had I been older and wiser, I would have understood that it's always better to play than sit."

BUCK MARTINEZ

"I knew I wasn't a baseball writer. I was scared to death. I really was afraid to talk to players, and I didn't want to go into the press box because I thought I was faking it."

ROGER ANGELL

easily the greatest baseball writer that ever lived

"Now that I know I can do it, there's a stress that goes away with that. Last year was kind of like, 'I think I can do it. I don't really know because I've never really done it before.' But now I know I can do it."

RUSSELL MARTIN

on catching R.A. Dickey's knuckleball

"Hey man, go out there and have fun, and relax, and do what you do."

JOSH DONALDSON

IN PRAISE OF THE IMPOSTORS

I feel this overwhelming urge to make myself a little vulnerable to you in the interest of the greater good. I want to speak candidly about impostor syndrome, specifically how it relates to my personal experience with the rather toxic realm of sportswriting.

For those of you who are unfamiliar with the term, impostor syndrome is a phenomenon that "occurs among high achievers who are unable to internalize and accept their success. They often attribute their accomplishments to luck rather than to ability, and fear that others will eventually unmask them as a fraud." (Thanks, American Psychological Association.)

Sports conversations are really excellent at fostering impostor syndrome. Despite the fact that I have been to hundreds of games, and have written thousands of words on the subject, I have often been made to feel like I'm not allowed to talk about baseball unless I know every single last possible thing about the game, going back to the very beginning of time. Like, when dinosaurs made bases out of boulders and bats out of fallen tree limbs.

"What do you mean you don't know that blah blah during the 1977 World Series Yankee Mike Torrez blah blah pitched his second complete game blah blah to win against the Dodgers in six blah blah?" (I just fact-checked the hell out of that, by the way.)

The silencing and conversational nay-saying that happens in sports culture is pervasive. You hear it at stadiums, and in bars, and at the family dinner table, and, quite frankly, it's damaging and it's poisonous. In the world of baseball writing, it is perpetuated by random critics, high-profile know-it-all blowhards, and lazy online trolls—people who have nothing better to do than sift through your words and your work to find teeny-tiny, obscure, irrelevant errors so they can yell "GOTCHA, YOU FRAUD!" in full public view. Not only does this bad attitude fail to foster a genuine love of the game, but in otherwise confident people it can instil a crippling sense of self-doubt that can be hard to overcome.

I can still recall the exact moment in 2012 when I decided I was going to write about baseball. I was watching a sports channel while running on the treadmill at my gym (I don't go there very often, so don't think this is a humble brag about my level of fitness), and I remember thinking there were so many men on-screen talking about the game. Man after man after man had an opinion on this, that, and this other thing. They were arguing, pontificating, and spreading their ideas and reactions to plays and developments like wildfire. It's not like I hadn't noticed the ubiquity of all-male panels in sports before, but watching this one in particular felt like the last straw.

Instead of simply lamenting the exclusionary nature of sports media, I decided to do something about it. A light bulb went on in my head and I thought, *Hey, maybe I can have an opinion about sports out loud and in public too.* I felt irrationally galvanized in a "fuck this" kind of way, and a few days later I used my media connections to wrangle up a press pass to a community event the Toronto Blue Jays were holding on-field at the Rogers Centre. (I totally acknowledge the privilege in that. As someone who worked at a magazine, and who has knowledge of the game and its players, I wasn't exactly starting at square one.)

Now, I don't necessarily recommend this kind of knee-jerk tactic, because by the time I walked through the concrete belly of the stadium, through the dugout door, and into an on-field scrum to put my audio-recording phone in José Bautista's face, I was floundering in a pit of my own barely concealed, dazed insecurity. One of only three women there, I could hardly make out a word the Silver Slugger said over my own internal monologue of *I have no idea what I'm doing and I really shouldn't be here.*

Having said that, I'm proud of myself for being brash enough to push so far out of my comfort zone, instead of spending the usual countless hours anxiously doubting myself or launching into a familiar self-directed speech designed to discourage me from doing something, like going to the event that day. (I'm pretty sure then–first baseman Adam Lind was totally on to my inexperience, though.) Ignoring those pesky (and false) feelings of not being sufficiently "qualified," I just went ahead and threw myself into a challenge I wasn't sure I could meet. The fact that I got through that first scrum gave me the confidence to go on and write about the game, and in the weeks and months that followed, I reached out to the sports editors I would have previously been too shy to approach. Some of them even decided to take a chance on me. With each new piece of writing, I found a firmer footing and a stronger voice, and I started to feel less and less like a fraud. I started to feel like I could belong.

I wish I could say that impostor syndrome is easily cured by a chat with José Bautista but, sadly, that's not the case. Despite my initial burst of uncharacteristic bravado and all the lessons I subsequently learned through hard work, sometimes I still feel like I don't know enough to write about this game. Yes, I'm continually enriching my knowledge by reading countless books and news stories. I listen to podcasts on the subway, and watch every matchup I possibly can while googling every single play and player on the field. And yet I remain prone to second-guessing myself, and having bouts of anxiety where I'm sure I've gotten something wrong. I meticulously fact-check every piece I write at least nineteen times before I file it, with every stat and sequence of events reviewed over and over again to ensure no one can call me out as incompetent. (This is not to say I don't make mistakes, or that people haven't taken it upon themselves to very publicly tell me how wrong I am.) On the extreme end of things, I am all too aware of how this degree of pervasive self-doubt can be crippling, or at the very least inconvenient and stupidly time-consuming.

Each time a new editor generously invites me to write about the game, I have a momentary panic of "can I really do this?" Maybe that's because I'm not a high-profile beat reporter for a major sports publication, or because I don't look, act, write, or dress like the majority of those who cover baseball. Every radio spot or public appearance is overshadowed by my own "why am I even here?" terror and anxiety, and when people very kindly tell me I am doing a good job, I automatically assume that it's because they feel sorry for me. (See? I told you I was going to make myself vulnerable.)

In 2016, I was invited to sit on a sports panel for a nationally broadcast radio show—a casual twenty-minute chat between sports "experts" that touched on three or so topics buzzing in the sports world during a given week. When I was asked to do it, I had that immediate internal response of "why me?" and then spent the next few days consumed by the fear that I'd sit at the table across from the host and be revealed as an impostor on live radio, while a drop of cartoon stupidity-drool rolled out of my gaping mouth. That, of course, didn't happen. When I got home, I listened to the recording and thought, *Oh good, not an idiot.* It was totally fine. Maybe it was even great. And certainly no one there, nor any of the listeners that day, accused me of not belonging on that panel of experts.

This self-doubt has afflicted me in many areas of my life, from taking on a new job to trying a new form of exercise to buying my first home. It has certainly hit me whenever I've started writing about any new topic, but for some reason I feel it most acutely in sports conversations. Maybe because of how much I love and want to serve the game, and maybe because sports culture has a nasty habit of making you constantly feel like you don't belong.

Perhaps it's totally unprofessional for me to reveal all these visceral sports expertise–related insecurities, but I think it helps newcomers to know that, despite outward appearances, not everyone is feeling A+ confident 100 per cent of the time. I also don't ever want to contribute to the same kind of "only so-called experts allowed" culture that declaratively anoints people "qualified" to speak, and that made me feel like there wasn't a place for me.

I think the misconception that you have to know every last factoid about baseball before you can talk about it not only makes writers and fans alike feel like impostors, but it also doesn't properly honour what is so beautiful about this game. Why would you want to know everything, anyway? Why would you ever want to stop learning all that baseball has to teach you? Every day, this sport has something new to offer: some new lesson or perspective, a new rule to unpack, or a new piece of historical knowledge to pick up. People approach it from so many different angles, and in turn offer myriad points of view on its greatness. The notion of there being baseball experts at all belies the truth that we're all trying, and learning, and capable of bringing something unique to the table. In baseball, as in life, not knowing it all is a benefit, not a detriment—one that keeps you open to new ideas, and helps you understand that it's ultimately rewarding to put yourself out there at the risk of making mistakes.

At the tail end of 2016's baseball season, I was invited to speak to a first-year creative non-fiction class. It was a fun, casual morning chat—the students were seated in a circle and encouraged to ask me any question they wanted about my career, the act of writing, and any struggles I've faced along the way. I was open about my own experiences with impostor syndrome, and got some laughs when I detailed past flustered reactions to interviewing baseball heavyweights like pitcher R.A. Dickey and Toronto Blue Jays play-by-play announcer Buck Martinez. Toward the end of the talk, one student sheepishly raised her hand and told me of her plans to be an art critic. She wondered how I cope with the nagging voice inside my head that keeps telling me I'm not good enough, because she was struggling with that same voice too.

I've been thinking about that brave young woman a lot since that day. At the time, I gave her a comforting, feel-good answer about faking it until you make it, and reassured her that everyone feels the same insecurity. Sure, it always helps to know that the majority of people—even so-called experts—are fumbling their way through just like you are. But I wish I'd told her the most important thing, and from now on I'll be sure to say it to fledging sportswriters, new fans, and anyone who's been plagued by self-doubt: The best way to deal with the voice that tells you that you're not good enough, or smart enough, or qualified enough, is to wake up every day and prove it wrong.

THE MAGIC OF THE NO-HITTER

Sometimes I think I'd like to live forever in the emotions conjured by the magical last inning of a no-hitter. I want to revel in the nervous anticipation of that last at-bat. I want to bask in the relief of that final successful out, in the warmth of that hug between a winning pitcher and his catcher, in the elation of that postgame celebration.

In the game of baseball, a no-hitter is very simply defined as a matchup lasting at least nine innings in which the opposing team is not able to record a single hit. The feat is more casually referred to as a "no-no," and by the end of the 2016 season, 295 instances had been recorded in Major League Baseball's history books. A single pitcher usually executes a no-no alone, but eleven in total have been aided in relief by the bullpen. In 1876, George Bradley of the St. Louis Brown Stockings executed the first official no-hitter on record, while the first of the "modern era" (beginning in 1900) was care of Frank "Noodles" Hahn of the Cincinnati Reds. Cy Young, the player for whom the most prestigious MLB pitching award is named, threw three in total, in 1897, 1904, and 1908. Hall of Famer Nolan Ryan holds the record for the most no-nos to his name, with seven in his twenty-seven-year career.

One of the most notable (and absurd) no-nos in major-league history occurred on June 12, 1970, care of Pittsburgh Pirate Dock Ellis, who unintentionally threw an entire no-hit game while high on LSD. (He had been confused about when he was scheduled to be on the mound.) “I started having a crazy idea in the fourth inning that Richard Nixon was the home plate umpire,” he later said of the game. “Once I thought I was pitching a baseball to Jimi Hendrix, who to me was holding a guitar and swinging it over the plate.” His effort wasn’t exactly the cleanest of baseball victories: his catcher had to wear reflective tape on his fingers so a drug-addled Ellis could read the signs, and the pitcher ended up walking a whopping eight batters before the final out. (On that note, it is possible to pitch a no-hitter and still lose an outing via walks, errors, or batters hit by a pitch—that’s happened five times since 1900.)

Part of what makes the no-hitter so special is just how uncommon it is. It’s sort of the white squirrel of baseball, the kind of thing you brag to your friends about witnessing first-hand at the park, although I have never actually seen one in person. (I came close during my first visit to

Detroit's Comerica Park in July 2013, when former Cy Young winner Justin Verlander was just a couple innings shy of executing the third no-no of his career.) There are a whopping 2,430 matchups in a regular season, but we're lucky to get just a handful of games without a successful hit. The most recorded in one season in the modern era is seven (that happened in 1990, 1991, 2012, and 2015), with the longest no-hit drought occurring between May 2004 and September 2006. That's why when word of mouth conveys that a pitcher is no-hit through, say, five innings, fans across the league converge quickly on the game to see if they can catch a glimpse of that mythical beast in action.

There is also no other baseball achievement so steeped in controversial, near-hilarious superstition than the no-hitter. Just as fans ritually wear lucky caps or unwashed team shirts to all the games that matter, many believe that naming a no-no while it's in progress is, well, a no-no. The accusation of "JINX" is often thrown at anyone—announcer, fan, or otherwise—who talks about its possible occurrence before it is completed. I've seen otherwise reasonable people convinced that a no-hit-ruining single was conjured by fans merely by speaking its name, as if any discussion is equivalent to staring into a mirror and saying "Candyman" three times. Instead, there are vague whispers in coded language: "*That thing* is happening over at the Phillies versus Cubs game," they'll say with a wink.

It turns out that belief in the baseball gods is never stronger than when there's the potential for a zero in the stadium scoreboard's hit column.

One afternoon in July 2014, I was watching the Blue Jays face the Red Sox from the desk of my magazine job, sneaking clandestine peeks at the baseball action on my computer screen between performing the arduous tasks of data entry and budgeting. Marcus Stroman was on the mound at the Rogers Centre during a rare weekday afternoon matchup. At the time, the pitcher was a twenty-three-year-old rookie, with only fourteen previous Major League Baseball games to his name. (In case you're wondering, in over a hundred years, rookie no-hit pitchers are an elite club of just twenty-two.) When Stroman's own no-hit bid went into the fifth, the magazine's editor-in-chief appeared ominously at the door of my office, sporting a stern, disappointed look on his face.

"What are you doing here?" he asked.

Knowing all too well my intense love of baseball and my convenient possession of season tickets, what he meant was if a no-no was possible, why wasn't I at the ballpark instead of at work? (Apparently he too was sneakily catching the game, listening in on the radio.) The Rogers Centre was only a fifteen-minute walk away—I could get there even quicker if I ran—so I had enough time to observe Stroman's ultimate greatness in person if it actually came to pass.

Without hesitation I abandoned my work, snuck out of the office, and sprinted to the stadium, only to find that they were no longer letting people inside. Unfazed, and driven by an overwhelming need to bear witness to something so elusive, I stealthily snuck in with the aid of an exiting fan, only to be stopped and reprimanded by a keen-eyed security guard. The only thing I could do was tell him the truth—my season ticket seat was only a hundred feet away, and I'd never forgive myself if I missed Stroman's first no-no. Understanding how important the moment was, he relented, smiled, and ushered me on my way.

In the top of the seventh, within minutes of me getting to my seat, Red Sox outfielder Shane Victorino hit a shallow leadoff single off Stroman into centre field, and the joy of the moment evaporated. That was the only hit Stroman surrendered that day, but the hope of seeing a legendary moment in his career unfold (and any subsequent insufferable bragging rights on my part) was lost. Toronto ended up defeating Boston, 8–0, and a game so close to making history simply disappeared unceremoniously into the books.

Despite my disappointment that day, I will always feel like my frantic, irrational, and maybe even law-breaking desire to get inside that stadium was entirely warranted. There's something spiritual about watching a player achieve the kind of greatness that a no-hitter promises. Sure, his comrades aid him in the process—outfielders dramatically catch surrendered pop flies, and infielders expertly snag the grounders that sneak into play. But a no-hit game feels like a glorious individual achievement; the victory of a single, indomitable athlete at the literal and metaphoric centre of the game; the enchantment entirely dependent on his mettle and his might alone.

The no-hitter is undoubtedly my favourite sports triumph, a rare and dreamlike event that pulls into sharp focus just why I love this game so damn much. While baseball naysayers often argue that its players are "not real athletes," a pitcher being able to throw an entire game without the opposing team getting to first base on a hit proves him to be superhuman. My admiration for pitchers—their fierce determination and physical endurance, their incredible mental focus, their ability to overcome fear, anxiety, and a harsh spotlight—tends to exceed my love for any other position, and the no-hitter is the apex

of the craft. And for me there are few moments greater than watching that man on the mound throw up his arms in both relief and victory, and throw his entire body into an embrace with his catcher.

If I'm honest, the no-hitter has the capacity to rejuvenate, and reaffirm, my belief that anything is possible, and it gives me the sort of heart-wrenching emotional catharsis that makes me feel a little better about humanity. (Yes, I always, always happily heave-cry when I see one.) I just love the thought of all the fans across the league finding out that, for example, Washington National Max Scherzer is no-hit through six, and quickly switching from their game of choice to tune in, all wanting to be part of the communal experience of watching something bigger than themselves unfold.

Incidentally, the great Max Scherzer has two no-nos to his name, both of which came in the 2015 season, and one of which was near "perfect," meaning no batter reached base at all. (Only twenty-three pitchers have thrown a perfect game, making it more unicorn than white squirrel.) Sadly, Scherzer's chances for perfection in June 2015 were controversially thwarted when he unintentionally plunked Pirate José Tábata with just one out to go in the ninth. (Some, including me, think Tábata leaned into it, or at the very least didn't make much of an effort to get out of the way.) No matter—with that win, Scherzer became only the sixth pitcher in Major League Baseball history to have two no-hitters in a single season. (And in 2016, he also became the sixth to have won the Cy Young in both the American and National Leagues.)

The first and only no-hitter of the 2016 baseball season was care of Chicago Cub (and later World Series Champion) Jake Arrieta. The April 21 game against the

Cincinnati Reds actually marked the pitcher's second no-hitter in just eleven starts, an incredible feat by any measure. Thirty-nine-year-old veteran catcher David Ross was behind home plate that day, and in fifteen seasons he had never previously caught a no-no. Further, "Grandpa Rossy" had already declared that season his last, making the whole affair all the more meaningful for the battery that achieved it, and for all the fans across the game of baseball who watched it.

"He kept squeezing me so tight," said Ross of the hug Arrieta gave him when the final out happened. "Hugging me with so much emotion. Trying not to cry."

I don't have any sort of special, personal, emotional relationship with Arrieta as a player, other than the fact I enjoy the Cubs and love that the pitcher once wore a moustache-printed onesie to a postgame presser. But that's exactly why the no-hitter is so compelling—it's an extraordinary accomplishment that somehow manages to pull away from everything that surrounds it. It makes you forget the standings, or how your team's bullpen is performing, or how an ump made a bad call, or how you currently hate the Baltimore Orioles. It becomes the main baseball event for all fans, regardless of their affiliation or affinity, which is why you'll often see opposing fans cheering too, because everyone knows a no-hitter is bigger and better than any one game. It's the rare instance when you can just admire the talent and the emotion on the field in front of you, without any of those pesky grievances or gripes getting in the way.

Maybe I love the no-hitter because it unifies us more than anything else in baseball can. If nothing else, it gives us all a chance to come together and cheer uproariously for that final, glorious out.

THE BEGINNING OF THE BEAUTIFUL END

Every year I think it's going to feel different, and every year it feels exactly the same. Somewhere during the last half-dozen outs of the Blue Jays' final game of the season, I get hit hard with a wave of painful emotion. It doesn't matter if my team is at the bottom of the East at the end of September or clinging to World Series hopes during an exhilarating October. It doesn't matter how much I prepare myself for what I know is coming. My gut always delivers the exact same ominous message.

"Baseball is ending," it warns. "It will be gone soon."

I don't think I have ever been more emotionally invested in a season of baseball than I was in 2016. Those seven months seemed more dramatic and more meaningful than anything I'd ever seen transpire on the field before, even if I didn't get the Blue Jays World Series win I wanted.

If I'm being honest, it was hard to be genuinely devastated when Cleveland's insurmountable pitching thwarted the Jays' chance to advance to the championship. Sure, when Troy Tulowitzki popped up into that last out of the ALCS and the Jays were eliminated, four games to one, I immediately turned off the broadcast and walked away. I didn't want to see any evidence of Cleveland's joy or Toronto's sorrow. I wanted to remember the season by its finest moments—an Edwin Encarnación extra-innings home run in the wild card game, a Josh Donaldson slide into home on an error for the ALDS sweep—and not by the close-ups of the forlorn expressions on the faces of the players I so faithfully supported.

But, in baseball parlance, I had to tip my cap to Cleveland's stellar efforts, and was able to move on from my disappointment to throw myself into the dramatic seven-game World Series that followed. I was even willing to entertain the idea that the two teams that made it to the fall classic were those who deserved to be there the most: Cleveland won their last championship in 1948, and the Chicago Cubs hadn't won in 108 years, or even appeared in the World Series in seven decades. The matchup was baseball romance at its finest—Cubs fans scrawled thoughtful messages to their lost loved ones in chalk on the brick walls of Wrigley Field, with one North Carolina Cubs fan even driving to his father's gravesite in Indiana so they could listen to the win on the radio together.

In retrospect, Game Seven was a perfect end to a very emotional season. The Cubs had miraculously come back from a three-game deficit to tie the series, and the final matchup at Cleveland's Progressive Field was nothing short of electrifying. Centre fielder Dexter Fowler kicked off the game with a home run for Chicago, becoming the first player to ever hit a leadoff Game Seven home run in World Series history. From there it was a gripping battle of well-matched rivals. Cleveland tied the game in the bottom of the third, but the Cubs scored two in the fourth. David "Grandpa Rossy" Ross became the oldest player to homer in a World Series Game Seven. There were runs aided by a throwing error and a wild pitch. Back and forth they went, until the score was tied at six, thanks to a Rajai Davis home run off Aroldis Chapman.

At the end of the ninth, in full theatrical style, the baseball gods brought the rain. Fans had to wait a seventeen-minute eternity for the downpour to cease, and by that point my husband was fast asleep in bed beside me. (He's become a fan, but not *that* much of a fan.) It was after midnight when the grounds crew finally removed the rain-delay tarp so the teams could again take to the field, and many viewers wondered how they would get through the following workday without falling asleep at their desks. When play resumed for the tenth, Chicago scored two in the top, and Cleveland fought back with one run in the bottom, making the score 8–7 for the Cubs.

With two outs in the bottom of the tenth, Chicago's Mike Montgomery was on the mound and Cleveland's

Michael Martínez came up to the plate. As millions of fans on both sides held their collective breath, the batter connected and produced an infield grounder shot out in the direction of Cubs third baseman Kris Bryant. "This is going to be a tough play," Fox broadcaster Joe Buck called as Bryant collected the ball and readied himself to toss it to first baseman Anthony Rizzo. "Bryant makes the play . . . It's over . . . and the Cubs have finally won it all." There are diehard Cubs fans who have waited their whole lives to hear those precious words, and I'll admit I was moved to tears watching those (no longer) "lovable losers" have their moment.

And the jubilant smile on young Kris Bryant's future-MVP face when he realized they'd won? That smile made a long, and yes, sometimes excruciating season totally worth it.

Through all my thinking, talking, and writing about this game, and after enduring the struggle, stress, and occasional pain it delivers, there is one fundamental question I keep coming back to: *Why do we watch baseball?*

Why do we obsess over matchups that can be exhausting, time-consuming, and even upsetting? Why are we happy to witness people we don't personally know take to the field and fight to the bitter end, even if that means waiting out rain delays and enduring extra innings? Why on earth do we irresponsibly stay up until past 1:00 a.m.

on a school night, all wired and anxious, to watch two teams battle it out? Why do we give ourselves over so completely to something that really is "just a game"?

As baseball's casual detractors so often like to remind us, baseball is boring, meandering, and even nonsensical. (Why does the American League have designated hitters while the National League has its pitchers hit? Why is it necessary for the catcher to tag the batter on an uncaught third strike?) The official rules are indeed needlessly complicated, and the language created around the game—with its batting around, beanballs, and bloops—can be opaque and impenetrable to even the most knowledgeable of fans. Baseball is an undeniably expensive habit that, with so many games in a season, takes up too much precious time in our already busy schedules. There's too much standing around. It's too unpredictable, too stressful, and the season drags on forever.

And yet with all the uncertainty and misery this game can bring, I will always believe in the genuine good it does for people. Without exaggeration, I have had fans tell me that baseball saved them when they most needed saving—during break-ups, health crises, mental health struggles, and grief—and that it gave them something to hold on to when there was nothing else to be found. The game provides the communal structure that so many of us desperately need when we feel isolated and untethered, and invokes a faith we sometimes can't otherwise muster in our daily lives. This game can be incredibly healing even when it is at its most heart-wrenching, and it provides a place where even the biggest cynics can muster gratitude in the face of loss.

"Why does this all make me so sad?" I asked my husband when he dutifully took me out for a meal and drinks after the Jays lost the ALCS, knowing that the day of my team's last game is, for me, one of the worst of the year.

"You're sad because you belong to some bizarre church where four months a year you're not allowed to worship," he thoughtfully replied.

No one will ever need to defend their devotion to baseball to me. This game pulled me up out of a ditch when I was at my lowest point, and gave me something precious to focus on, day in and day out, while I got better. It was my anchor and my lifeline, my lighthouse in the storm. It made me believe in magic again, reaffirmed my faith in others, and helped me see hope when I thought there was none.

Baseball induces in me a visceral, full-gut longing. In a world that demands we be upright and well put together all the time, the drama of the game allows for—and even encourages—passionate outbursts. When I see reliever Jason Grilli roar and pump his fist after a much-needed out, or see closer Roberto Osuna make the sign of the cross after executing a game-winning strike, it's as if a pressure valve has been released; I am finally allowed to let go. During every high-intensity play, pitch, or at-bat, I cry, and I squirm, and I yell full-throated without fear of who hears me. I am raw, vulnerable, and unashamed. I am my most authentic self. I let the feelings that baseball evokes control me, even though, because of what I have endured in my life, I am usually afraid of giving up control. And I've happily and wholly surrendered myself to this game, letting it take me where it wants (both emotionally and geographically), even when my primary instinct is to never let my guard down.

With my hands in the air and my voice hoarse, I am so grateful for that freedom to be fully myself, messy feelings and all—if only for a short period of time.

Late one Friday night in November, about three weeks after the Chicago Cubs won the 2016 World Series, I walked home after having dinner with a close friend. At the time, my city's sidewalks were layered with the yellow, orange, and red crunch of autumn's fallen leaves, and a fuzzy scarf was pulled close around my neck to beat the chill. By then, that incredible championship series between Chicago and Cleveland had become a beautiful, if fuzzy memory. And as I walked homeward in the cold, next year's pilgrimage to spring training felt painfully far away, with so many inches of snow to trudge through before I could put on my ball cap again and get back to the stands where I belonged.

I meandered along some quiet neighbourhood side streets, leaving the giddy noise of the city's bustling bars and restaurants further and further behind me. When I was close to my house, I decided to make a small detour to my local community baseball diamond. There were only a few people in the surrounding park, including some kindly midnight dog-walkers tossing a ball and a few cheery couples sharing a goodnight embrace. The diamond's dramatic overhead lights were on and bathed everything in their glow, the brightness creating a welcoming, churchlike atmosphere in the night.

I impulsively strayed from the adjacent sidewalk, walked through the gap in the chain-link fence behind home plate, and ended up in the spot where the pitcher would stand on game day. This particular playing field was certainly nothing fancy—just a configuration of gravel and faded chalk lines designed for the community's Little Leaguers and casual adult beer leagues. The dirt under my feet was soft, an expanse littered with puddles thanks to an earlier rainfall. The infield grass was coated with a thin layer of frost that warned winter was on its way. With my hands stuffed in my pockets for warmth, I looked into the outfield, and watched the silhouette of someone's overexcited Labrador running to catch a ball where the right-field wall would be.

For a few calming moments I just stood there taking it all in, the only sound the whistle of a light wind and the rise and fall of my breath. As I scanned the points where a local team would install their bases, I felt like a weight had been lifted, and I basked in the temporary escape from the seemingly endless harm and chaos of the world. There were no pitchers or batters, no call of the umpire or beer vendor, no roar of the crowd—but there I was, comforted nonetheless.

Even that empty diamond, shoddy with disuse now that the weather had changed, could offer me a little light in the darkness. I may always lament the terrible yet predictable end of baseball, and worry about what the cold months ahead will bring, but I try to remember this: Baseball can indeed break your heart, but, without fail, it will always find a way to make it whole again.

WELCOME TO THE LONG DARK

> "Most people crave autumn, but August's finale guts me. Always the heartbreaking close of summer, no matter the weather, always the beginning of the end of baseball season, which is the beginning of the long dark."
>
> HOLLY M. WENDT

When you love baseball as much as I do, you measure your days and weeks and months in the game. You structure your deadlines and appointments and holidays around making sure you can get to the ballpark while your team's in town. You get anxious in the lead-up to big matchups, and you get bored on your team's days off. You need it. You crave it. It dictates your life.

And if, come September, you're lucky enough to get meaningful games from your potentially playoff-bound team, your entire month is up in the air. If things go particularly well, you find yourself telling people you're not sure if you can see any of them until November. You cut short a long-planned family vacation because your team "Owned the East" and you have to be back for the postseason. (Sorry, Aunt Joanne.) You ask an editor for an extension because your team is going to the ALCS. (Your editor, it turns out, completely understands.) You have tickets to an event that falls on the same date as Game Two, and your companion says he'd totally get it if you bailed. (The two of you end up blowing off the event to take in the last four innings at a local bar.)

Baseball becomes the master of your schedule and your mood, and in the process it exhausts you. While your team's destiny is being played out on the field, you are a barely functional human being, having forgotten how to perform basic adult tasks: your social life is in shambles, your diet and sleep suffer, and your laundry piles up in a way you're a little ashamed of. (I call that the "postseason floor-drobe.") But through it all you are always grateful to the game. Because who, in their wildest dreams, ever gets to love something this much?

And then, with one last October pitch, it's all gone.

Thus begins what I have taken to calling ominously "the Long Dark"—the vast, vacant space between that final out and that optimistic day down south when pitchers and catchers report for spring training. (It's about 120 days, in case you're wondering.) For me, everything in the bleak expanse in between is frustrated waiting—it's an abyss, a black hole, an all-encompassing fog that hope can't penetrate. Whenever I lament the end of baseball in what I know might sound like a melodramatic way, someone inevitably says, "Well, there's always winter ball," but I've long found personal solace at the ballpark. If I can't be in one, you can't convince me there's something to look forward to.

I usually attend about three dozen live games during the regular season. I've gone to the ballpark to celebrate my birthday, and I've gone to help console someone when she'd had a bad week. I've gone with strangers who became friends, and I've met up with my dad there hundreds of times. I've been with deeply devoted fans, and I've been with people who'd never been to a ballpark before. I've gone when I simply couldn't comprehend the world's terrible tragedies, and I've gone when my anxiety was so bad I could barely breathe. I've caught a ball game when, hit by bad news, I didn't know what else to do, and when it was the only thing I wanted to do. I go to the ballpark over and over and over again, from March until October, and I would go more often if I could. Because to me, baseball is home like nothing else.

I've never really understood why the ballpark is the one place where I feel safest, happiest, and most like myself. It doesn't even matter which ballpark it is—the foreign fields found at the end of hasty road trips, the tiny, gleeful stadiums of spring training, the neighbourhood parks of Intercounty League. Even watching Little Leaguers tossing a ball at my local diamond or a drunk group of friends running the bases after the bars close buoys me.

I once had an experience in New York where I walked around the city for a full day coated in inexplicable dread, unable to isolate its source. Those who have anxiety disorder will know the feeling well—logically, the panic doesn't make sense, but the physical sensation of doom is all too real. It's like living under a suffocating shadow that refuses to let up. No matter how many times you're told to "calm down" and "relax," the worry doesn't go away. I was supposed to go to a Yankees game that evening—my first ever in New York—but I wasn't sure I could do it. The idea of my anxiety-stricken, agoraphobic self taking the subway to Yankee Stadium during rush hour seemed absurd, yet I braved the journey anyway, packed in between the bodies of yelling, sweaty fans in ball caps on their way to 161st Street station.

But I swear to you, the moment I walked into that majestic ballpark, with its bright white columns and banners printed with the faces of legendary players, the fear was gone. It was lifted away by that low hum of fan devotion and that great field of Kentucky bluegrass, the boys bursting from the dugout and the crack of the bat. Better than cognitive behavioural therapy or pharmaceuticals, the ballpark cured me just like it always does.

Hell, I don't even like the Yankees.

Because of how therapeutic it can be, there have been many instances during a live baseball game when I have thought to myself, *Don't forget this and how good it feels*. It could be anything from the simple enjoyment of being outside on a bright sunny day with my cap on and my shoulders bare, to the elation of witnessing a walk-off home run or a complete-game shutout, knowing how lucky I am to have been there to see it. I know that during the bleak, wintery moments, these ballpark memories will sustain me, and I'll desperately need to summon them as proof that things can and will get easier and better. That everything will eventually renew again.

Memorize this moment, I think. *Remember how happy it makes you.*

When people ask me what I find so compelling about this game, I offer some loose theories about justice, and fairness, and community. I talk about how it's the closest I've been able to come to a religious-style faith, and how I think it's healthy to believe so strongly in something outside of yourself, something you can't control. But for the most part, I can't pinpoint a real reason for that intense and immediate feeling of calm that comes over me when I walk through a stadium gate.

While unpacking my own devotion to the Church of Baseball, I often wonder if it might be better not to write about the sacred, secret places in our lives that keep us whole. Writing is a compulsion, but perhaps I shouldn't write about the ballpark, just as I don't write about the people who are closest to me or about the things I want to keep private and safe. Of course I want to understand what it is about baseball's sights and smells and sounds that put me so at ease, but given how much the game has changed and, yes, how it even saved my life, maybe it doesn't matter why. Maybe what matters is that I've finally found something that does.

Once that last game of the season has been played and winter comes again, I'll do my very best to get through the Long Dark. I'll watch baseball montages at my desk while it snows outside, cheering for the incredible plays of the past and getting teary-eyed for all those home runs that have already happened. I'll flip through the photographs of great baseball moments that I've lovingly saved on my phone, and I'll proudly wear a team T-shirt under my scratchy sweater.

And while the ground outside my house is still frozen over, I will set a countdown clock to that sunny, hopeful day come February, when pitchers and catchers report in Florida and Arizona, the grass is green, and the Long Dark finally ends. I will gaze at the date on the calendar that represents my first live game of the season, and wait patiently for the return of the comfort and solace that being at the ballpark provides. And I'll be thankful that, even in the depths of winter, baseball always gives me something to look forward to.

ACKNOWLEDGEMENTS

Thanks to the wonderful, hardworking team at McClelland & Stewart and Penguin Random House Canada who helped to make this book possible, including Joe Lee, Kim Hesas, Valentina Capuani, and CS Richardson. Thanks also to Linda Pruessen and Sara Black McCulloch, with a special nod to the unbelievable copyediting and fact-checking heroics of Gemma Wain.

I'm especially grateful to my editor, Anita Chong, whose patience, talent, and vision are unparalleled. Anita is both my elite Cy Young–calibre starting pitcher and my steadfast extra-innings closer, and I am forever in her debt for pulling me through until the final out. Thank you to my agent and friend, Samantha Haywood, who championed the lofty idea of me writing a baseball book, and who, like always, selflessly supported me throughout the process.

Earlier incarnations of these essays appeared in *The Walrus*, the *Globe and Mail*, *Vice Sports*, *Blue Jays Nation*, *Canadian Notes and Queries*, *The Classical*, *The Barnstormer*,

Torontoist, *Ravishly*, *Hazlitt*, *Open Book Toronto*, and the *Baseball Life Advice* newsletter. (Thanks, subscribers!) I'm ever grateful to editors Andrew Stoeten, Scaachi Koul, David Hains, Mark Medley, Erica Lenti, Kelli Korducki, Susan G. Cole, Jordan Ginsberg, David Roth, and Caitlin Kelly for taking a chance on my sportswriting, and to Matt Galloway and the team at CBC Radio's *Metro Morning* and *q* for generously giving me a voice in the sports conversation. Special thanks goes to Matthew McKinnon, whose keen editorial eye and unwavering support—in both writing and life—could easily be credited with the fact that I ever wrote about baseball at all. (I've forgiven you for thinking baseball is boring, Matt.)

Thank you to the fierce and talented women who make up my day-to-day sportswriting support system: Julie DiCaro, Jessica Luther, Shireen Ahmed, Brenda Elsey, and Lindsay Gibbs, you've all helped and guided me more than I can ever say. Thank you to John Lott for all your open-hearted wisdom and guidance, and to R.A. Dickey for your endless humanity and kindness. Thank you to Teva Harrison, David P. Leonard, J.P. Robichaud, Adam Green, Brittney Teasdale, Beth Hitchcock, Vivek Shraya, Ruhee Dewji, Miranda Newman, Jared Bland, Heather Cromarty, and Natalie Zina Walschots for being a part of my best days and for getting me through my worst, and to my mom and dad for their unwavering love and encouragement. Thanks most of all to Spencer

Saunders, who sacrificed countless hours to supporting me, my work, and my love of this game. There's no place I'd rather be than at a ballpark with you.

And, of course, thank you to my ever-growing baseball family. Thank you to anyone who has ever enjoyed nine innings with me at the stadium, and to everyone who has shared a devotion to the Church of Baseball. It's been a genuine pleasure to cheer with you—here's to many more beautiful Octobers.

NOTES

A number of the player quotes in this book were collected during media events and postgame clubhouse scrums, and reported by outlets such as Sportsnet, theScore.com, ESPN, MLB.com, the *Globe and Mail*, the *National Post*, the *Toronto Star*, and the *Toronto Sun*. Wherever possible, individual outlets and interviews have been noted.

The epigraph on p. vii is from *Foul Balls* by Alison Gordon. Copyright © 1984 Alison Gordon. Published by McClelland & Stewart, a division of Penguin Random House Canada Limited. Reproduced by arrangement with the Publisher. All rights reserved.

The epigraph to "More Than Mean" is from George F. Will's opinion piece "Baseball's storyteller, our friend," *Washington Post*, September 2, 2016.

The R.A. Dickey quotation that serves as an epigraph to "The Runner on Third" is taken from my interview with the author, "The literary life of R.A. Dickey," *National Post*, March 28, 2013.

The epigraph to "José Fernández, 1992–1996" is from Anna McDonald's "The reinvention of José Fernández," ESPN, September 25, 2016.

The epigraph to "The Long Dark" is from Holly M. Wendt's "Nothing Happens at Coors Field," *The Classical*, September 25, 2013.